Wildeor

The Wild Life and Living Legacy of Dave Foreman

Wildeor

The Wild Life and Living Legacy of Dave Foreman

Edited by Susan Morgan and John C. Miles

Essex Editions

Wildeor: The Wild Life and Living Legacy of Dave Foreman

Editors: Susan Morgan and John C. Miles
Copy Editor: Katie Shepard
Book Designer: Michael Grossman

Front Cover Photo: Dave Foreman face shot, Glen Canyon Dam © Dave Foreman Collection
Background Cover Photo: Cedar Mesa, Utah, May 2018 © John C. Miles

Published in the United States by Essex Editions.

ISBN: 978-1-7335190-4-5

Library of Congress Control Number: 2023903643

Essex Editions
Post Office Box 25
Essex, New York 12936
www.essexeditions.com
contact@essexeditions.com

Table of Contents

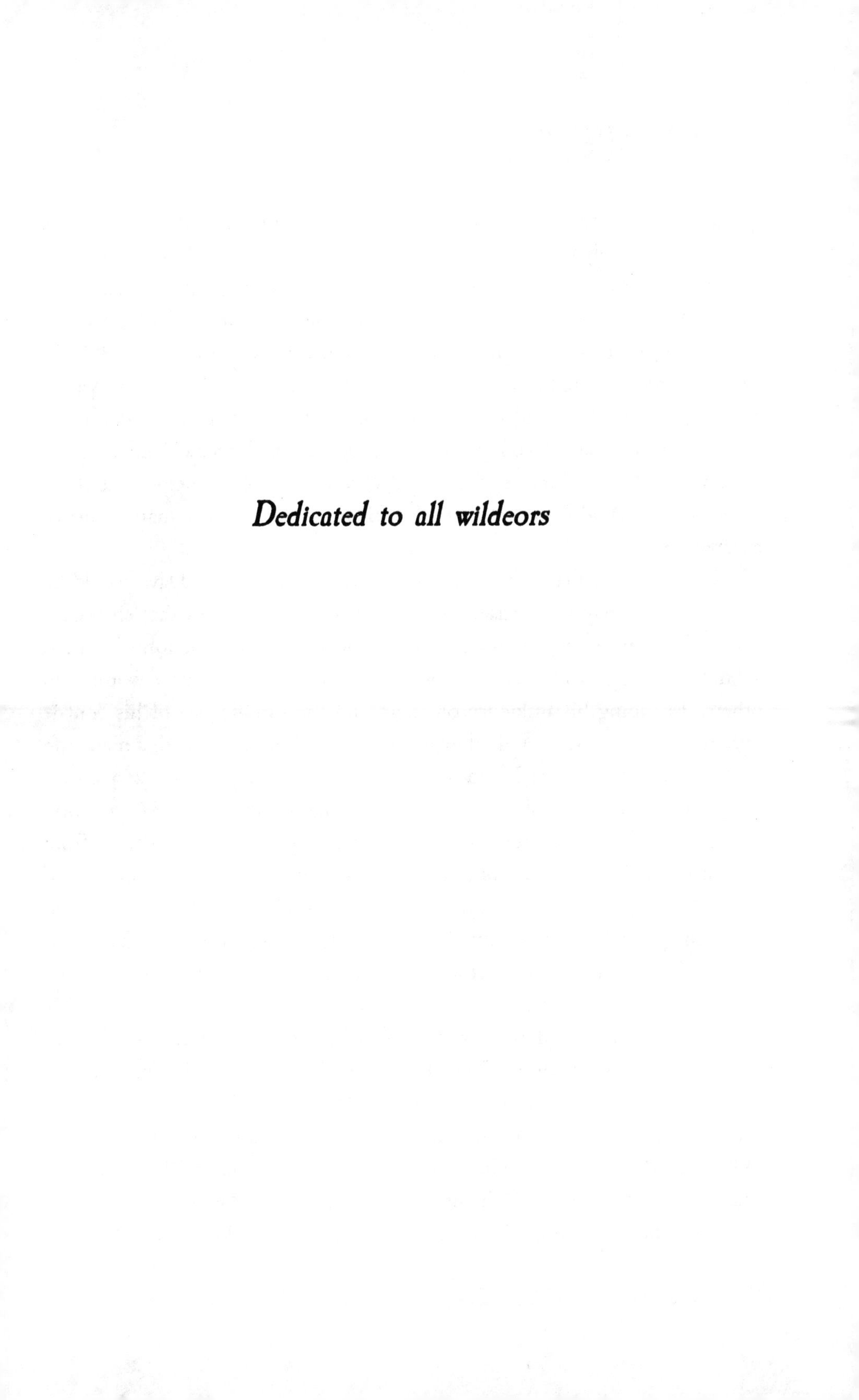

Dedicated to all wildeors

Foreword

Dave Foreman, eloquent and powerful advocate for wilderness and wildlife, affectionately known by his many friends as Smilodon, Bumblefuss, and Uncle Dave, passed away on September 19, 2022, surrounded by friends and family. As Susan Morgan, a friend and colleague of Dave for half a century, recounts in her essay that opens this memorial volume, on his last day Dave expressed regret that he had not had the time to write his memoir, which he intended to title "Wildeor," an Old English term that means "free willed beast," a quality that Dave repeatedly said defines wilderness. Wilderness, to him, was land where Nature made the decisions, or most of them, rather than *Homo sapiens*. Wild creatures could live there as free from human influence as anywhere.

Susan assured Dave that a volume titled *Wildeor* about Dave would be compiled, and here it is. Susan asked every friend of Dave's that she could think of, in consultation with Dave's great friend and colleague John Davis, to submit a memorial to Dave, and most responded. Some used more words than others, describing his influence on them and the significance of his contributions to conservation, and all expressed their admiration for this man who had accomplished so much and influenced so many people who carry on his work today. We consider this little volume a *festschrift* which *Webster's Third International Dictionary* defines as "a miscellaneous volume of writings from several hands for a celebration," and we certainly have here a celebration of life. A *festschrift* is also often compiled to honor a scholar, and while Dave did many things in his seventy-five years—farrier, activist, outdoorsman, writer, orator—he was also a scholar, making the idea of a *festschrift* for him appropriate in that sense too.

We have organized the contributions here somewhat chronologically, though not only so. Some contributors worked more with Dave during his years as a field representative for The Wilderness Society, or when he was a rousing leader of Earth First!, or when he and others formed The Wildlands Project, or when he was the founder and leader of The Rewilding Institute. Some worked with him through all these stages. However and whenever they encountered him, Dave always was an influence, as all writers testify. He had charisma, an eloquence, a stage presence as speaker and actor, that made an indelible impression. He articulated ideas that many could not, and he often did so with vehemence. Some called him "Preacher Dave," and he could certainly preach. As I have worked on this project with Susan, editing and organizing, my great respect for and understanding of this complex fellow has grown. I did not know him very well until late in his career, though I had read his writings for decades and knew of his considerable influence on the history of conservation. I am honored to be able to help celebrate his legacy.

– John C. Miles

Dave and Terry, 2014 © Dave Foreman Collection
50th Anniversary of the Wilderness Act Conference, Albuquerque

Dave Foreman Remains My Hero, My Truth Teller, and My Conscience

Terry Tempest Williams

Editor's Note: This essay by Terry Tempest Williams was published in *Anchor to Windward, A Loving Tribute to Dave Foreman* in 2015 by the New Mexico Wilderness Alliance (now New Mexico Wild) "with gratitude for the contributors to the Dave Foreman Tribute Fund at the New Mexico Wilderness Alliance." It is published here with permission of New Mexico Wild.

To say Dave Foreman is a hero is too easy—he is. To say Dave Foreman is a transformative figure within the conservation movement, well, it's a fact. But to say Dave Foreman is our collective conscience in the name of all things wild is getting closer to the truth of things, that is where Dave Foreman's greatness of spirit resides.

On the 50th Anniversary of the Wilderness Act in Albuquerque, New Mexico, the place Foreman calls home, he said to a packed audience of young people, "My advice to all of you who are considering having children, don't! The Earth doesn't need any more of us."

He forever remains the truth teller, the radical-conservative, the contrarian, the Coyote Extraordinaire, the one who dares speak, howl, cry and cry out on behalf of wilderness.

"Our environmental problems originate in the hubris of imagining ourselves as the central nervous system or the brain of nature. We're not the brain, we are a cancer on nature."

With all due respect, Dave is not a "cancer on nature;" he is a blessing. I am glad he is here. Whether it has been his work with The Wilderness Society; or one of the co-founders of Earth First!; or reimagining his own work through The Wildlands Project alongside his paper monkeywrenching as a writer, Dave Foreman has left an indelible mark on the American political landscape not only as an environmental activist, but an eco-philosopher, and one of the greatest orators of our time.

Who can ever forget Dave Foreman's charisma at the Earth First! gatherings or his presence at the Land, Air, and Water Conferences repeatedly with David Brower at the University of Oregon? How many times did we howl with him at the end of each of his speeches, or see in our mind's eye in times of indecision—the raised fist of Dave—followed by a raucous "No Compromise in Defense of Mother Earth!" so passionate, so confident, so committed to a love of the wild?

Dave Foreman remains my hero, my truth teller, and my conscience.

I can't tell you when I first met Dave Foreman because the stories that preceded our meeting told to me by Mardy Murie who loved him, Doug Peacock who respected him, and Ed Abbey who counted on him—made him familiar to me, part of the family, brought into my life as a vibrant voice for freedom. When we did meet, he felt like a brother, always warm, always fierce, and always ten steps ahead of the rest of us regarding strategy and spirited public actions on behalf of public lands.

But what I have come to love and respect most about Foreman is the size of his heart, the depth of his intellect, and the honesty of his struggle—to keep fighting, to keep inspiring those around him, and never give in or give up on his core values of wilderness—in the face of personal pain, both physical and emotional.

Courageous leadership comes with a cost, highlighted by the fact that the United States government wanted nothing more than to silence him, destroy him, even if it meant entrapment. The FBI thought by shackling him with an ankle brace that registered his every move during his too-many-years on parole that they would defeat him. They only made Dave Foreman smarter, braver, more cunning against their watch. By calling one of our finest patriots a felon for defending our homeland with a soul commitment to keeping our public lands, or public commons wild and free—the Federal Government inspired Dave Foreman to be more powerful, not because he survived their abuse, but because he went deeper into the intellectual underpinnings of our nation's soul-sickness in its relentless drive to destroy the very land that has created our national character.

Today, Dave Foreman is one of our elders with white hair and a white beard, well-earned with his characteristic, charismatic twinkle in his eye. We are right to fear him with his fist raised high, as his "night work" is now done in broad daylight each time he speaks, picks up his pen, or walks in the wilderness he loves.

I love the man, and I'm grateful to call him my friend. His life is an ongoing Howl-le-lujah!

Terry Tempest Williams
Castle Valley, Utah

Terry Tempest Williams is a writer, educator, conservationist, and activist, author of eleven books and editor of many more. She has received many honors and awards. An uncompromising activist like her friend Dave Foreman, she left the University of Utah which had awarded her an honorary doctorate and where she had taught for 13 years when the University requested revisions of her contract in 2016. This came after she and her husband had successfully bid on federal energy leases in Utah to protest federal energy policy there. She stood on principle against a community unhappy with her actions, as Dave also often did. She has, for many years, been Writer-in-Residence at the Harvard Divinity School and has taught at Dartmouth College. In 2019, Terry was elected to the American Academy of Arts and Letters. Her address to the gathering for the 50th Anniversary of The Wilderness Act in 2014 moved the audience to tears and cheers. She, like Dave but with a very different, often gentle and emotional style, is a very moving orator.

An Inspiring Fifty Years

Susan Morgan

After fifty years of friendship and collaboration, I had grown accustomed to Dave. Looking back, he had always been close by, an inspiring influence and reliable support as a friend and colleague in the important work we were doing. Perhaps I took it for granted that he and Nancy would be with us for a long time, and losing one, then the other produced a monumental personal shift for me and many of us in his conservation community.

How fortunate we are to have had this brilliant, complex, gifted, creative visionary in our lives, bringing all those good ideas and great good humor, which increased the prospects of making a positive difference. Rowdy, too, and Nancy, his dedicated conservation partner, joined in the good fight. He despaired about what was happening to the wild world but didn't give up.

When I got to his house in Albuquerque on the morning of September 18, I sat down next to Rox, and Dave said, in his usual forthright way to both of us, "Someone had better take notes. I'm not going to be here much longer, and you guys had better get this right." So, I grabbed my computer and leaned in for orders.

Though he would sleep now and again, he would wake and talk to friends and family, warmed by the gathering, which he considered like those in traditional and native cultures. When Dave was awake, he was clear as a bell. He regretted dying "so soon" because he felt he still had a lot to do. Even when he lost consciousness, he would squeeze my hand when I read him emails and messages from his friends who were unable to be with him then.

Then he slipped away, and in December, John Miles and I went back to Dave and Nancy's house and spent two days with Christianne Hinks. We read files in his office and went through boxes in the office and garage and reboxed it all. As we know, he saved everything. Over 100 boxes were shipped to the Denver Public Library to be housed in the Dave Foreman Conservation Collection where researchers will be able to access primary information about his life with The Wilderness Society, Earth First!, The Wildlands Project, The

Rewilding Institute, and more. We helped a little, but it was Christianne who made this happen. DPL was so eager to have Dave's files that they reached out to initiate the process, explaining they already had a few boxes and had started a Dave Foreman Collection, and then they footed the complete transportation cost, which was considerable. Four new archivists there will be working on his papers soon, if they aren't already. Their eagerness to have Dave's papers is indicative of his stature in the conservation history world.

Dave lamented too many losses in recent years: Nancy, Kim Crumbo, Ed Abbey, and others. I told him that last day that he wasn't helping, which made him snicker.

He seldom lost his sense of humor, specializing in self-deprecating stories and emails. Friends and Rewilding folks were entertained by accounts of fights with his computer, which he threatened to shoot many times, and recipients would respond in kind, enough that I was able to assemble a sizeable "Nonsense" file. If he figured out the problem, he would let us all know and celebrate his prowess with a good bottle of something. At the end of his life, he exclaimed in victory that he wouldn't have to mess with computers anymore.

Dave would send around delightful, detailed accounts of his medical woes or accidents. Falling out of one of his trees twice while constructing an outdoor cat run, leaning out of a raft too far and falling in, sliding down a ladder in the backyard. After patching him up through the years, Nancy forbade certain activities. Years ago, she had to carry him out of a ravine in Death Valley at night after he had gone out to obey the call, and the following Christmas everyone in the Morton family sent him a flashlight.

He wrote us all to find out where he could get some chainmail after scratching his arms gardening and tripping in his house, and a friend sent him a good supply of night lights and bubble wrap. He passed along recipes, giant ground sloth being one of the most memorable. Marinate it for at least a week in green chili and then add Dave's spices before cooking slowly until well done. Mammoth was another possibility. Mice, too, of which he had a plentiful supply and had shared myriad accounts of fighting them in his garage with hot sauce and Clorox.

Upon request, he sent out directions for making another crack for the Glen Canyon Dam. We received a full family explanation of why his first language was "Texan." On and on. He signed his emails Smilodon Dave, Uncle Bumblefuss, or Uncle T Rex.

At this writing, *Wildeor*, a testimonial collection or *festschrift*, is well underway. The response to our solicitation for contributions has been wonderful. Reading what others have expressed reminds me that he was involved in so many more actions and projects that I only knew about from afar. I have been swept away by the perspectives in this little book, one that Dave requested we assemble for him. I wish he could read it.

Mostly, though, thinking about him after all this time brings home once more that we've known a most remarkable person, a man for all time. Someone who has changed the course of conservation history. So, we'll keep him close, and we'll get it right.

Remembering a Father Tree

John Davis

The wilderness community and the global rewilding movement pay tribute to a founding father. In his three-quarters of a century, Dave Foreman changed and expanded the way we do conservation in North America and inspired conservation activists and biologists to think big, wild, and connected throughout the world.

Since Dave Foreman's death from interstitial lung disease on September 19, the last group he founded, The Rewilding Institute (rewilding.org) has been flooded by fond remembrances and glowing tributes to his vast influence. A common theme in these grateful messages is: *Dave Foreman changed my life. I saw him give a speech (in whatever the city or university or wilderness conference) and from then on, I dedicated my life to wild things and places.*

Some of these messages from Dave's close friends and colleagues have compared him to a giant tree in an old-growth forest. This metaphor I find particularly heartening, for as we all know now, big dead trees, standing or fallen, are as life-giving as are green trees. Dave is now like a mighty oak fallen in an old-growth gallery forest along the Gila River, southwest New Mexico, nurturing new generations of trees and their defenders, and guiding us as we work to protect and restore the Mogollon Wildway, linking the Gila Wilderness with Grand Canyon National Park, as part of the Spine of the Continent Wildway.

My own little conservation story hints at Dave's influence. In college, I saw Dave and his fellow Earth First! co-founders Bart Koehler and Howie Wolke give hellfire & brimstone wilderness speeches at a rally for unprotected wildlands. The week I finished college, I hitchhiked across the country to volunteer at the *Earth First! Journal* office in Tucson, Arizona. I thought I'd do a year of service, then go back to school. Dave's vision was too compelling. I could not leave. For nearly four decades now, I've been trying to help Dave

John and Dave © Doug Tompkins
Dave Foreman stands with his younger friend and follower John Davis on a wildlands-scouting trip across Patagonia with Doug & Kris Tompkins and Denise Wilson, circa 2000.

implement his vision for rewilding North America. Thanks to Dave, I've lived a life incredibly rich in experiences, if occasionally lean in resources. Dave's numerous friends and colleagues constitute a powerful community—like an old-growth ecosystem—of wildlands activists, biologists, and writers; and I've had the honor of meeting many of them, often at the home of Dave and his beloved wife Nancy Morton (affording me the opportunity to wash dishes for some of the finest people in the world!).

I was fortunate to get to know the soft side of Dave, as well as the more distant, heroic side. As a living legend, Dave could be intimidating. He had an encyclopedic memory for conservation and natural history and for public lands geography. He could name and describe virtually every species exterminated by our forebears in North America. He stopped timber sales on more National Forests than most Americans ever even have a chance to walk. With Howie Wolke, he completed the most comprehensive US roadless area inventory ever conducted (the subject of their book *The Big Outside*). As a friend, though, and for many of us as a mentor, too, he was generous, funny, warm, and one of the best storytellers we had ever heard. Dave's wife Nancy was a conservation leader in her own right, among many other distinctions serving as president of the New Mexico Wilderness Alliance. Dave always made clear, in their home, Nancy was boss, along with their beloved cats. Dave spent weeks designing and building a cat-arium at their home in Albuquerque, which allowed the cats to go outside but prevented them from hunting songbirds.

Part of Dave Foreman's great legacy will be courage. Dave was fearless in the face of bulldozers threatening ancient forests, critics falsely accusing him of not caring about people, and government agents who infiltrated Earth First! when the Reagan administration perceived us as a threat to economic growth. Dave taught us to speak boldly for what wild Nature really needs.

He was not a revolutionary, however. Indeed, Dave was deeply conservative, believing that protecting our natural heritage and learning to coexist with our wild neighbors are core values shared deep-down by most thinking, feeling people. Dave always argued that conservation should be non-partisan—that folks from all political parties and walks of life should embrace wildlands and wildlife conservation. In recent decades, Dave usually voted for Democratic candidates but only because the Republican Party had turned against its early deeply conservative values and became hostile to public lands and wildlife protection.

Dave Foreman was famously controversial at times. His book *Man Swarm: How Overpopulation is Killing the Wild World* was a blunt look at how excess human numbers, in terms of population and consumption, are driving the extinction and climate crises. (Editors' Note: Dave Foreman, *Man Swarm and the Killing of Wildlife* was published in 2011 by Raven's Eye Press. A second edition, with a new subtitle published in 2014, was Dave Foreman with Laura Carroll, *Man Swarm: How Overpopulation is Killing the Wild World*, published by Live True Books.) Dave took much heat through the years for confronting human overpopulation as a fundamental problem. Dave felt (and many of us who worked with him agree) that conservationists' and environmentalists' retreat from population planning advocacy was among the worst mistakes we ever made. Some others of Dave's writings were almost uncomfortably frank in how they criticized mainstream, foundation-supported conservation and environmental groups. Dave was sometimes an iconoclast, like his older friend Ed Abbey had been; and every movement needs that, discomfiting though their words can be.

Perhaps the most enduring part of Dave Foreman's legacy will be the rewilding movement. Dave coined the term 'rewilding' about a quarter century ago. His short definition of 'rewilding' was 'wilderness recovery;' but he explained it at length in his landmark book *Rewilding North America*—the closest thing to a blueprint for how to achieve what are now called Half Earth goals on the most affluent continent. Dave grumbled often and laughed occasionally at how his neologism 'rewilding' had been adopted by manifold interest groups, ranging from drumming circles, to folks seeking spiritual enlightenment, to alternative medical practices teaching gut biome health. He occasionally chafed at the suggestion of some conservationists that rewilding start at small-scale levels, like restoring native plants to our yards. He practiced such healing local work himself but did not see it as rewilding. Big, Wild, and Connected were the basic descriptors of rewilding for Dave; and he wanted to see projects protecting big core reserves and protecting or restoring the full range of native wildlife, including apex predators like wolves, big cats, bears, raptors, and sharks.

Like most brilliant people, Dave Foreman was complex and paradoxical, though, and I believe in the main, he was pleased to see work for other species expanding under the rubric *rewilding*. The final test for Dave on whether work lives up to the rewilding label was, does it served wild creatures—'wildeors,' or self-willed beasts, as Dave liked to call our furred, feathered, finned, and flowering neighbors.

Dave gave his storied life to protecting and restoring a wild Earth, for wildeors of all sizes, from small songbirds to giant redwoods. The mighty oak that was Dave Foreman has fallen to nourish new generations of rewilding leaders. Dave Foreman did not, in the flesh, live to see the day Wolves, Pumas, and Grizzly Bears in Mexico would have unbroken lineages north along the Spine of the Continent into Canada, but may the young rewilding leaders he will inspire achieve such big, wild, connected visions here and around the world.

John Davis is the Executive Director of The Rewilding Institute and editor of *Rewilding Earth*. He serves as a wildways scout, editor, interviewer, and writer for TRI and rounds out his living with conservation field work, particularly within New York's Adirondack Park, where he lives. John serves on boards of RESTORE: The North Woods, Eddy Foundation, Champlain Area Trails, Cougar Rewilding Foundation, and Algonquin to Adirondack Conservation Collaborative.

John served as editor of *Wild Earth* journal from 1991-96, when he went to work for the Foundation for Deep Ecology, overseeing their Biodiversity and Wildness grants program from 1997-2002. He also served as conservation director of the Adirondack Council from 2005 to 2010.

My Support of Dave's Philosophy

Kirk C. Robinson, Ph.D.

As a boy growing up in northern Utah, I became intensely interested in the early exploration of the American West by Lewis and Clark, Jim Bridger, and others. I devoured books about Native Americans and mountain men, imagining myself living a wild and free life alongside them. Through the years, I have made dozens of backpack and river trips into many of the West's remotest and wildest places, instilling in me a deep love of wilderness and wildness.

I was in my final year of a Ph.D. program in Philosophy in Ohio when I first became aware of Dave Foreman and Earth First!. Like so many others, I was attracted to Dave's fiery persona and his bold wilderness vision. It was also during this period that what I loved came under explicit threat in the form of James Watt, Ronald Reagan's mendacious Secretary of the Interior. I knew then that I had to live in the Rocky Mountain West and work to protect its wild places. This conviction has shaped my life ever since, eventually leading me to found Western Wildlife Conservancy and to work on the Wildlands Network "Heart of the West Wildlands Network Design" with colleagues Jim Catlin and Allison Jones of Wild Utah Project.

My recollection is uncertain, but I may have met Dave for the first time at a conference on carnivores in Denver in 2000. Over the years I have seen him and heard him speak at various conferences and gatherings. However, I only spent personal time with him on one occasion. Some years ago, my colleague Michael Robinson and I met Dave and his wife Nancy Morton for dinner at a Mexican restaurant somewhere in Albuquerque. The delicious food was accompanied by a wide-ranging and spirited conversation. Afterward, Dave gave me a big bear hug in the parking lot and thanked me for my conservation work as we parted. It was a moving gesture. I also saw Dave at the Wilderness Act 50-year anniversary celebration in 2014 in Albuquerque.

Courtesy of Kirk Robinson
Kirk is the Executive Director of the Western Wildlife Conservancy, Salt Lake City, Utah

His closing keynote speech was Dave Foreman at his eloquent, incandescent, and humorous best. These experiences are among my treasured memories and continue to inspire and motivate me.

While I was never personally close to Dave, I admired him from afar and have always thought of him as both a kindred spirit and the leader of the cause I became devoted to.

My essay in honor of Dave, "The Balance of Nature?," which was published online in *Rewilding Earth* (see: rewilding.org/the-balance-of-nature/) presents some of my personal philosophical reflections on issues pertaining to wilderness and wildlife. I believe they align closely with Dave's views and will be pleased if they provide an extra layer of support for them.

Kirk Robinson is the founder and Executive Director of the Western Wildlife Conservancy. He lives in Salt Lake City, Utah. Prior to founding Western Wildlife Conservancy, Kirk earned a Ph.D. in philosophy and taught courses at universities in Montana and Utah for 15 years. His favorite activities are exploring the wildlands of the American West and trying to learn to play bluegrass and fiddle tunes on acoustic guitar.

Big Brother Dave

Roxanne Pacheco

Little did I know that afternoon when I took my big brother to the doctor on August 31 that he would be dead three weeks later of a mysterious lung infection that caused his oxygen levels to drop to extremely low levels. Oh, how my heart is broken that I will never see him again or have a conversation or go on another trip with him. But I will always have memories of a brother bigger than life.

I was born on August 6, 1955, in Yuma, Arizona, the third of three children born to Skip and Lorane Foreman. Dave said I was the best birthday present he ever got; his birthday was October 18. Momma and I were in the hospital for three weeks or so because I was a premie. Dave wasn't allowed to visit, so he wrote momma a letter asking, "Why did you name her Rocks and Sand?" Thus began a long, loving relationship between the two of us.

I can't imagine what my life would be without his influence on me. He taught me that all of life had its own value and that you had to fight for what you believed. When we were young, we attended the Church of Christ where my parents were members, and that is where Dave learned to speak and engage an audience, one of his many talents. I remember an occasion when I was very young: We were standing outside of the church, and I smashed some ants on the sidewalk with my shoe. He was horrified and said, "Why the hell did you do that? Don't you think they deserved to live?" I still feel guilty about that, but it taught me an important lesson.

Dave always had a love of wildlife, wild things, and wild places. When he was young, momma would read to him every night. He did not want nursery rhymes. He wanted stories about nature and animals. Over and over, she read to him from two volumes of the American Museum of Natural History, *American Wildlife Illustrated* and *Wildlife* the *World Over Illustrated.*

My parents were not campers or outdoor adventurers, but we would go on day picnics and long road trips that introduced us to the country. We were living in Washington State when Dave was a boy scout around 1961. One of the requirements for a merit badge he wanted to earn was to go on a family camping trip, so our parents, who always encouraged us to follow our dreams, borrowed a bunch of camping gear and we set off on our adventure. It rained the whole time, and my parents were absolutely miserable. But Dave, Steve, and I couldn't get enough, hiking in the woods, cooking over a fire, and when it cleared up, looking into the night sky. Thus began my love of the outdoors and adventures. In following years, Dave took me on many adventures, crazy rapid river trips, Earth First! Rendezvous, hiking, and climbing mountains. When my children were born, he also introduced them to the adventure of being in the wild.

In August of 1988, Dave and his wife Nancy took my oldest son Gerard on a backpacking trip in the Gila Wilderness when he was twelve years old. Here is an account of one adventure on the trip from *Confessions of an Eco-Warrior*:

> Because of the unusually heavy rainfall that summer, the West Fork was roaring. The rushing water was above my knees, but the first crossing wasn't too difficult. Armed with alder hiking sticks, Gerard and Nancy picked their way across the ford. We realized this would not be a leisurely stroll down the canyon, but reckoned it would be passable without mortal danger. As we forged our way downstream, though, the current ran faster, the crossings grew deeper, the trail became a long, muddy puddle, and the rain continued to pelt us. Soon the river had climbed to my waist and was trying to strong-arm me downstream. I moved my sleeping bag from its usual place at the bottom of my pack to the top. Nancy—who had once lost her pack and been stranded on a rock mid-river in northern California's Ishi Wilderness, having been tossed off her feet by a snow-melt surge—gritted her teeth and fought her way across the fords. But Gerard, a short little squirt, couldn't wade the torrent without getting his entire pack (and sleeping bag) soaked. This meant I had to make three trips through each ford; one trip for my Kelty, one pack, and then a third piggybacking Gerard and his pack.
>
> To make our requisite five miles a day, we had to trudge most of the daylight hours. Our enthusiasm for birdwatching and fly fishing

washed out of us with the crossings; everything we had was going into making our way across those damn fords and then walking fast enough down the soggy trail through the continuous thunder storm to stave off hypothermia. It was senseless to try to stay dry. Lightning smacked the rim and rock pinnacles above us. Pour-offs usually dry turned into cascading waterfalls. As the West Fork pounded me into humility, Gerard developed an admirable aptitude for fording the river. As I grew weaker, he grew stronger. Transferring his sleeping bag to the dryer refuge of my pack, he half-skipped and half-swam across the current with the aid of his alder staff. Good thing, too.

By the third day, I no longer had the stamina to muscle my way three times across each ford. Once, when old wilderness hands Nancy and Dave were at a loss as to how to get across a ford where the current ripped under a fallen cottonwood and created a potentially fatal situation, Gerard found a safe crossing for us upstream. Late on the third day as we hobbled into the parking lot, I smiled at my nephew and teased him, "I bet you can't wait to get back to Big Macs, video games, and TV." Dripping like an alley cat that had been flushed down a sewer, he looked at me, looked back up the rocky canyon of the West Fork to a black-bellied thunder storm growling overhead, and said, "Let's go back."

Rest in peace, my beloved brother. As long as I'm on this Earth, I shall do my best to make sure your legacy lives on.

– Rocks and Sand

Roxanne Pacheco lives near the bosque of the Rio Grande in Bernalillo, New Mexico. She loves spending time in the New Mexico wildlands and has been active in state conservation issues through the years. She has supported her brother Dave in his various organizations and with the sales of his books, and she has been the treasurer for The Rewilding Institute since 1992. Roxanne owns a tax and accounting company, Bosque Taxes.

Dave Finds His Mission

Dave was always proud of his modest roots, hillbilly he would call them, and proud of his Scotch-Irish heritage, a family that arrived at the end of the frontier migration into eastern New Mexico. He would tell his friends that he came from pinto-bean farmers near Clovis on the Llano Estacado. He was proud also of his upbringing in the Church of Christ, and though he lost his religion in college, Dave retained excellent preacher-like oratorial skills all his life.

A military family, the Foremans moved a lot. Dave survived the constant changes but shy, sensitive, and smaller than others was a late bloomer. He was a misfit in the Marine Corps, but later in life was proud of the dishonorable discharge certificate hanging on the wall of his office. He remembered fondly his years in Zuni, where his father was stationed in the Air Force. An Eagle Scout, and proud of it, he enjoyed his first wilderness adventure when his troop, from another of his father's Air Force postings in Blaine, Washington, took a long backpacking trip into the Glacier Peak Wilderness. He often, later in life, spoke of that trip and the impression the mountains and big trees made on him.

Dave loved the outdoors, and in the early 1970s was enthusiastically backpacking and river running in the Southwest. A college friend, Dave Seeley, introduced him to several guys, Jack Loeffler, Bill Brown, and Jimmy Hopper, who had organized the Black Mesa Defense Fund to fight a strip mine planned for Black Mesa on land sacred to the Navaho and Hopi peoples. Not only was a mine in the works, but the coal would be transported 273 miles as slurry to the Mohave Generating Station which would require much of a very scarce resource in that part of the world—water. Loeffler writes of this, "Here we were, tiny coteries of early 'radical' environmentalists who had taken on Goliath's granddaddy—a behemoth so enormous and so well-funded, so politically connected, so anointed with corporate blessing... that we were doomed at the starting line." Dave volunteered to help with this lost cause, and it proved a turning point for him. In *Coyote and Towndogs*, Susan Zakin writes of this effort that the Black Mesa Defense Fund "was to the Sierra Club what John Coltrane was to Bach. It was a hell of an introduction to the environmental movement."

Dave moved back to Albuquerque from a refuge in the Jemez Mountains, organized an office there for River Defense, an offshoot of the Black Mesa campaign, and enrolled in school to prepare for what he had discovered he wanted to do with his life—become a career conservationist. He joined the New Mexico Wilderness Study Committee, who seemed to him a bunch of old geezers doing necessary work, and found himself coordinating that group's response to a review of the Gila National Forest plan. He threw himself into this work, also serving as Wilderness Chairman of Students for Environmental Action of the Albuquerque Environmental Center. At issue were competing proposals for Gila Wilderness expansion, the Forest Service proposal was deemed very inadequate by a coalition of conservation groups. He became so busy that he dropped out of school and made a name for himself organizing environmentalists to comment at Forest Service hearings, doing his share of commenting and starting to develop the preacher skills he would later become famous for. This work brought him to the attention of The Wilderness Society, and soon he found himself invited to Washington, D.C., participating in a week-long lobbying seminar in January of 1973. Meeting and impressing some powerful environmentalists who expanded his horizons, he was invited to go to work for the Society.

He took the job as TWS Southwest Representative responsible for New Mexico and Arizona. The Wilderness Society paid him big bucks—$250 per month plus $50 for expenses. Dave was thrilled. Also attending that seminar were wilderness activists Bart Koehler and John Miles, recruited from Wyoming and Washington State respectively. Susan Morgan was the TWS Denver office educational coordinator and was assigned to coordinate Dave and other field reps, one of the most effective grassroots conservation programs in conservation history. Susan and Dave became good friends, destined to work together on and off for the next half-century.

TWS Southwest Rep was the perfect job for Dave. The Southwest was his country, and he set about expanding his already considerable knowledge of the geography of the region, its conservation history, and current conservation issues there, poring over maps and committing them to his prodigious memory. He continued to work on Gila Wilderness issues throughout his tenure as Southwest Rep, and myriad other issues such as wilderness proposals for Bandelier National Monument, the Blue Range, and Bosque del Apache, among others. He used methods conventional at the time—writing letters to Congress, especially the delegations in his domain, testifying at hearings, organizing local campaigns, and creating and presenting slideshows to educate about conservationists' positions. In a 1979 article in *The New York Times*, journalist Molly Ivins writing from Reserve, NM, reported on wilderness battles, quoting logger, rancher, and miner opposition to any wilderness designation. A Glenwood rancher said, "Wilderness designation means immediate death for the timbermen and certain but slower death for the ranchers." He added, "Environmentalist is a dirty word around here. I've had ranchers tell me that Dave Foreman is lucky to be alive." (*NY Times*, "New Mexico Town Sees Battle on Wilderness Area as Fight to Survive," 1-28-1979.)

By the time this article appeared, Dave was back east in Washington, DC, transferred there in 1978 to coordinate the field rep program under TWS Acting Executive Director Celia Hunter. He was out of his element. Susan Zakin quotes Celia Hunter: "He'd be fine in New Mexico, in the local rough-and-tumble of politics at that level. But he doesn't like this whole slick thing of how to buy your way into power you don't earn." He was not a good fit, especially when turmoil in TWS sent Hunter back to Alaska and Bill Turnage was hired as executive director. Dave was a free-wheeling westerner, a Buckaroo as he and his western field buddies called themselves, while Turnage was more of a buttoned-down businessman. Ultimately, in 1979, Dave decided to move on.

Remembering Dave Foreman

Camilla Fox

Sitting on a plateau
Overlooking the Jemez, Ortiz and Sangre de Cristo Mountains
Cottonwood trees blowing in the evening breeze
Crickets pulsing
The big dipper—Ursus Major appearing over the dark night sky.
And I take in the message I have just received—
Dave Foreman has left this world.
I was to see him yesterday,
—to say my goodbyes in Albuquerque.
But he was going down, not feeling well.
I thought about what I would say to him,
My gratitude for his vision, his courage, his singular focused passion and dedication
To rewilding this continent.
To raising awareness, consciousness, action
For Earth First
For Wilderness
For the Wild Ones.
He set the course for so many of us
Who carry on the fight
To re-wild North America
To bring pack apex predators,
To reconnect broken landscapes,
To bring back the wild.

And as I write these words
An eruption of coyote song,
A coyote serenade in the Pinyon pine juniper savanna in Cerrillos, New Mexico.
How fitting,
The call of the Wild
For Dave—in his homeland.
A reminder that the wild will persist
Will keep resisting persecution,
Destruction.
They and we "Wildeors" will carry on your legacy,
Will keep howling & fighting for
Big, Wild & Connected
Continental Conservation
—your bold vision of
A fully functioning, healthy & diverse
Wild Earth.

RIP Dave - now united with Nancy & Crumbo, 9.19.22

Camilla H. Fox is the founder and Executive Director of Project Coyote—a national non-profit organization based in Mill Valley, California, that promotes compassionate conservation and coexistence between people and wildlife through education, science, and advocacy. She has served in leadership positions with the Animal Protection Institute, Fur-Bearer Defenders, and Rainforest Action Network and has spear-headed national, state, and local campaigns aimed at protecting native carnivores and fostering humane and ecologically sound solutions to human-wildlife conflicts. With 25+ years of experience working on behalf of wildlife and wildlands and a Master's degree in wildlife ecology, policy, and conservation, Camilla's work has been featured in several national and international media outlets. She has served as an appointed member on the U.S. Secretary of Agriculture's National Wildlife Services Advisory Committee and currently serves on several non-profit advisory boards.

Absolute Truth and Honesty

Lynn Cottin

My memories are scattered now that Dave has passed. They come back to me in bits and fragmented pieces. Of course, could be age! But I was much more focused when I knew he was going to that final roundup and hitting the trail for good. I don't have momentous historical words of wisdom that dropped from his lips in that fateful time; my strongest thoughts and recollections of a lifetime are of his character and his beliefs in keeping the wild *wild.*

Mostly I remember his huge bear hugs where he'd lift me off the floor like a leaf when he'd come to Washington, DC, back in his Wilderness Society days for meetings or assignments. I always knew when Foreman was in the building.

I also remember morning calls from Dave and late-night ones from Bart. They were a constant.

Dave would tell me about his life in Glenwood, how a puma or a mountain lion liked to hang around his house, so he had to be sure to keep the cat inside (his or Debbie's, not sure). How he was going for a run, or just coming back from one, and what things he'd seen along the way. I remember one graphic conversation about how the plumbing was stopped up and it was time to go dig a latrine. He certainly did have a fascination with outdoor toilets and groovers! My sister recently sent me a pic she took when we were on the '79 raft trip with him and a gang of his pals where he graphically demonstrated the art of the groover. I'd totally forgotten that picture and it's probably better that it's not in the archives.

Late-night calls were from Bart, in some saloon, waxing poetically about the state of this or that. My boyfriend would roll over at 2:00 AM and mumble, "who's that?" I'd say, "Bart," and he'd respond, "say hi" and go back to sleep. I always counted on talking to one or the other several times a month.

One of my fondest memories is sitting on the floor of Dave and Debbie and Tim's house in Arlington, writing letter after letter to senators and congresspersons about saving Alaska while drinking a can of warm beer and getting horrible writer's cramp. Felt like we each wrote a million letters that night!

What I remember most about Dave, after he had given his most gospel-like sermon to gatherings of potential contributors and supporters, was his absolute truth and honesty, his belief that what he was fighting for was absolutely necessary and right and needed doing. It might be almost too late but, he was convinced, it was never hopeless. He had a southern sermon Baptist preacher-like quality, and the twang that would come into his speech was adorable. Of course, anyone who ever heard the Easter Story can attest to that. No one could tell it like Dave.

I will miss how happy he was about the Solstice, delighted to be on the San Juan or in any wild setting, how passionate his beliefs were, never wavering, how tickled he was when, not so long ago, I sent him little nightlights to put around the house so he wouldn't fall downstairs. Or upstairs. How heart-warming it was to pick up the phone, and hear him booming, "hey darling."

I surely do miss him.

Lynn Kraynak Cottin, a recent Oregon transplant from Albuquerque, New Mexico, moved to NM from Washington, DC, where she worked with Dave and the rest of The Wilderness Society crew in the 70s. She is a Master Gardener and supports conservation/educational/musical/artistic causes and is happiest outdoors, especially on any given river, or looking for fossils, minerals, shells, or plants to identify. She loves birdwatching but has trouble identifying one little brown bird (LBB) from another.

Earth First!

Dave Foreman left The Wilderness Society in May of 1980 for several reasons. He had tried the Washington, DC, life and decided it wasn't for him. As Celia Hunter had observed, he was better suited to politics on the ground rather than on the Hill, and he knew it. He was a westerner, and even though loggers, ranchers, and miners hated environmentalists and there was risk in being one out there, he decided that was where he could best do good work for conservation. Secondly, The Wilderness Society was changing with a new executive director, whom he regarded as more businessman than a passionate defender of wilderness, a career-oriented "technician" who didn't get his boots dirty, who seemed more interested in running a smooth and prosperous organization in Washington, DC, than in doing the hard work in the field. He could see that the new boss, Bill Turnage, would hold the field reps on a tighter leash than had Celia Hunter, and he was, as someone observed, better at giving orders than following them. The "buckaroos," as the cadre of field reps called themselves, enjoyed a free-wheeling style that Dave could see was not likely possible in the new regime, if indeed field staff even continued to be part of the organization.

Most importantly, as he observed in his 1991 book *Confessions of an Eco-Warrior*, he saw problems emerging from the increasing professionalism of conservation groups like TWS (admitting that he was himself being professionalized). He wrote, "a number of problems can be attributed to this increasing professionalism, chief among those problems being the concentration of strategic and tactical decision-making in a small elite, and an emphasis on pragmatic politics instead of ethical fundamentals." In the decade since he had become a conservationist, he had learned the importance of grassroots organizing by passionate defenders of wilderness. He was convinced that leaders of this work, like him, needed to love the outdoors, wild nature, and wilderness, and be passionate believers in the necessity of protecting them. He had concluded that the goal of conservation had to be the recognition of intrinsic value of every living being on Earth (the ethical part.) That was not what he saw in the big Washington, DC-based conservation organizations. New approaches to conservation work were needed, including a return to the ethical foundations of the field he saw in the thinking of Aldo Leopold among others, though he didn't know, when he left TWS, what these approaches might be.

Dave hooked up with others who shared his views and ideas, and out of that convergence came Earth First! as is described in tributes here from Bart Koehler and Howie Wolke. Disgust at what they saw as minimalist recommendations from RARE II (a second Roadless Area Review and Evaluation), brought Koehler, Wolke, Mike Roselle, and Dave together in 1979. These guys took a trip to Mexico's Pinacate Desert, where they drank a lot of beer, explored the wild landscape, and discussed what should be done. As Howie tells the story, the idea of forming an organization emerged after the trip when Dave exclaimed they should call it "Earth First!," and so it was.

In *Confessions* Dave explains how the mission of the outfit was conceived.

> Maybe some of us began to feel, even before Reagan's election, it was time for a new joker in the deck: a militant, uncompromising group unafraid to say what needed to be said or to back up with stronger actions than the established organizations were willing to take. This idea had been kicking around for a couple of years. Finally, in 1980, several disgruntled conservationists—including Susan Morgan,

formerly educational director for The Wilderness society; Howie Wolke, former Wyoming representative for Friends of the Earth; Bart Koehler, former Wyoming representative for The Wilderness Society; Ron Kezar, a longtime Sierra Club activist; and I—decided that the time for talk was past. We formed a new national group, which we called Earth First! We set out to be radical in style, positions, philosophy, and organization in order to be effective and avoid the pitfall of co-option and moderation that we had already experienced.

What, we asked ourselves as we sat around a campfire in the Wyoming mountains, were the reasons and purposes for environmental radicalism?

- To state honestly the views held by many conservationists.
- To demonstrate that the Sierra Club and its allies were raging moderates, believers in the system, and to refute the Reagan/Watt contention that they were "environmental extremists."
- To balance such antienvironmental radicals as the Grant County commission and provide a broader spectrum of viewpoints.
- To return vigor, joy, and enthusiasm to the tired unimaginative environmental movement.
- To keep the established groups honest. By stating a pure, no-compromise, pro-Earth position, we felt that Earth First! could help keep the other groups from straying too far from their original philosophical base.
- To give an outlet to many hard-line conservationists who were no longer active because of disenchantment with compromise politics and the co-option of environmental organizations.

- To provide a productive fringe, since ideas, creativity, and energy tend to spring up on the edge and later spread into the center.
- To inspire others to carry out activities straight from the pages of *The Monkey Wrench Gang* (a novel of environmental sabotage by Edward Abbey), even though Earth First!, we agreed, would itself be ostensibly law-abiding.
- To help develop a new worldview, a biocentric paradigm, an Earth philosophy. To fight, with uncompromising passion, for Earth.

The name Earth First! was chosen because it succinctly summed up the one thing on which we could all agree: That in *any* decision, consideration for the health of the Earth must come first.

In a true Earth-radical group, concern for wilderness preservation must be the keystone. The idea of wilderness, after all, is the most radical in human thought—more radical than Paine, than Marx, than Mao. Wilderness says: Human beings are not paramount, Earth is not for *Homo sapiens* alone, human life is but one life form on the planet and has no right to take exclusive possession. Yes, wilderness for its own sake, without any need to justify it for human benefit. Wilderness for wilderness. For bears and whales and titmice and rattlesnakes and stink bugs. And… wilderness for human beings. Because it is the laboratory of human evolution, and because it is home. (*Confessions*, pp. 17-19)

Over the next 10 years, Dave became the public face, eventually the "elder statesman" of Earth First!.

During ten tumultuous years, Dave was a key organizer of Earth First!, wrote prolifically and edited *Earth First! Newsletter* then *Earth*

First! Journal; traveled the country as the EF! Roadshow with Johnny Sagebrush (Bart) holding rallies and giving rousing speeches; wrote books (*Ecodefense: A Field Guide to Monkeywrenching*, 1985; *The Big Outside: A Descriptive Inventory of the Big Wilderness Areas of the United States*, with Howie Wolke, 1989); conceived and helped stage "gonzo" guerilla theater ("cracking" Glen Canyon Dam); and joined protests (as Andy Kerr describes in this collection). He was busy, controversial, and ultimately the target of an FBI takedown as an "example" to the rest of the "radical ecoterrorists" that angered loggers, ranchers, miners, government agencies, even "respectable" conservation organizations.

Finally, in 1990, believing that Earth First! was moving in directions he could not support, he moved on. He and his wife Nancy, in their resignation letter, wrote:

> We will continue with the fight. Dave plans to begin work on thoroughly revising and updating ECODEFENSE into a Third Edition. And, along with others who emphasize biocentrism, we will be starting a new organization to work on concrete proposals for ecological wilderness identification, preservation, and restoration . . . It is time to regroup, refocus our energies, confuse our enemies, and do whatever we can do best to impede the destruction of our precious Earth.

Dave Foreman & Me: Grizzled Galoots in Cahoots

Bart Koehler

From "The Earth First! Li'l Green Songbook:"

> *"Johnny Sagebrush (or Bart Koehler) is an outlaw country buckaroo songwriter and performer. In a two-minute song he can capture more magic, passion, and meaning than I can in an hour-long harangue. He is the original bard of Earth First! Bart Koehler is also my best friend and the only person I know who is more full of BS than I am (although he'll tell you the same thing about me)." – Dave Foreman*

Back in the day there were tales to tell. Dave and I were best buddies since early 1973 when we were field reps for The Wilderness Society (TWS). It was our mission to help build bedrock grassroots support for protecting Wild areas and the best hunting and fishing watersheds on our public lands by law.

In the late 1970s, the new boss at TWS turned his back on working with grassroots groups. Soon after that, we were becoming disillusioned with what mainstream environmental groups were willing to settle for. Dave and I left TWS and mainstream environmental activism and, with a few other folks, co-founded Earth First!. Dave and I toured the US with the Earth First! Road Show where he gave rip-snortin' speeches and, under the stage name of "Johnny Sagebrush," I played guitar and sang sing-alongs to get crowds warmed up. Dave's speeches were humdingers for sure and always got the crowd enthused, invigorated, and whooping and hollering. And several times we shared the stage with the legendary Edward Abbey.

Dave and Bart, 2019 © Julie Koehler
Pleasant days on a houseboat on Lake Foul

After a couple of years, life on the road had taken a toll. Sure, it was fun placing a 300-foot crack across Glen Canyon Damn and leading rallies against James Watt. We enjoyed our 1982 human blockage and rally against Getty Oil's attempt to drill the wild heart of the Gros Ventre Range, which helped win protections via the 1984 Wyoming Wilderness Act. But I yearned to return to helping grassroots groups gain Wilderness Area protections via acts of Congress. So, I went back to mainstream conservation work, first in Wyoming, then in Alaska, later in Nevada, Idaho, Virginia, Montana, North Dakota, New Hampshire, and even more states.

Dave continued his brilliant endeavors under the banner of Earth First!. Then, after leaving Earth First!, he and several other very talented people co-founded The Wildlands Project, The Wildlands Network, The Rewilding Institute, and the New Mexico Wilderness Alliance. He remained an incredible and invigorating speaker, as well as writer and philosopher extraordinaire, and all of those organizations did excellent, effective work under Dave's leadership and mentoring. Many he mentored continue his work today. Now Dave is gone. But his vision and courage live on and will inspire many, many people during the years ahead. He truly was one of a kind. And he will be truly missed, but we have lots of memories.

Dave couldn't tell his right foot from his left. When we were doing the road show, we devised code language to help us navigate downtown streets. We agreed that when we were on the highway or crowded city street, we'd operate as though we were rafting or canoeing the Rio Grande Canyons between Texas and Mexico heading down river. Texas was a left turn and Mexico was a right one. Of course, we had to add a further layer of complexity to the road show since Dave's Volkswagen van would only start when we pushed and rolled it downhill from a high point. Then he'd pop the clutch in second gear and we were on our way. If we'd forgotten to park it in just the right way, we'd be stuck! That's how Dave's trusty vehicle got its American Indian Name: "Parks on a hill."

Dave was also tone-deaf. When we'd be engaged in a road show, he would always enthusiastically sing and belt out the words. We had to make certain that he never had a microphone anywhere near him while he was singing. We always had a good laugh over this, but he was serious when he longingly spoke about a tone-deaf band he'd like to be part of and get to name "The Mule

Bray Chorus," honoring the string of mules that he had back when he was a muleskinner prior to working for TWS.

In 2014, there was an ironic form of justice for us two outlaws, at least as we were perceived by some, the FBI among them. We were featured presenters at the national celebration of the 50th Anniversary of the Wilderness Act held in Albuquerque, New Mexico. Dave gave a rousing, spirited keynote speech, and I sang a few of my original songs as part of the opening ceremony. As usual, Dave received a standing ovation from hundreds of fans with tears in their eyes. For my last song, the audience was standing and singing along acapella in a standing-room-only crowd of 1,200 people. Wildly spirited stalwarts shedding tears for all things good and Wild. Forty-one years after the start of our friendship, these two old galoots were still in cahoots and had returned to their Wilderness roots.

The last time I saw Dave, we were up in Escalante Canyon in the Cathedral of the Desert. Because Lake Powell was shrinking and treasured places that had been inundated with water were now becoming uncovered, we were able to wind our way to Katie Lee's favorite waterfall and her special place in Glen Canyon (Katie was a folk singer and a river guide in the Glen Canyon). The acoustics in this enclave were fantastic. Beholding this scene and the rewilding of this special spot, we started singing a prayerful version of a song I'd written decades ago, "Were You There When They Built Glen Canyon Damn?" Extraordinary echoes flowing out of Escalante Canyon brought tears to our eyes and filled our hearts with song. This cathedral was born again.

So here we are today, some forty years after the infamous Road Shows, and finally Dave gets his wish of having the Mule Bray Chorus and Mother Nature's Marching Blues Band play and sing at this celebration of his life. We who are putting the music together will do our best to make sure that the Mule Brays sing and play their hearts out in such a way that Dave and so many of our heroes can hear us from up high in the mountain bluebird blue sky and star-filled night.

Bart Koehler is one of the most respected wilderness leaders in the United States. He worked 19 years with The Wilderness Society, and from 1999-2011, he was Director and then Senior Wilderness

Campaign Director of TWS's Wilderness Support Center in Durango, CO. After being the coordinator of the American Wilderness Project for several years, Bart has been trying to learn how to retire while being on the board of directors of several wilderness conservation groups across the country. Following his calling over the past fifty years on a rough and rocky public lands protection trail, Bart has helped bedrock grassroots groups put our democracy to work for good and wild causes with the results being over 11-12 million acres of permanent protections.

Dave and bulldozer, 1988 © Terence Moore, Dave Foreman Collection
Practicing for the Next Encounter

Stand in Front of that 'Dozer

Lyrics by B.N. Koehler

Chorus:
Stand in front of that dozer
Stand in front of that dozer
Stand in front of that dozer
Till it turns around

Waitin' in the moonlight with a chill
Down my back
Heard a bulldozer comin' down the track
Rollin' and a roarin' with a clickity clack
I sure do hope that he turns back

(Chorus)

The dozer's comin' closer I can see it son
Movin' fast at us like a shot from a gun
I think I'm getting' nervous, who said this was fun?
It's him or me, I hope he turns and runs

(Chorus)

Now it becomes a simple test of will
The man yells "Move out or you'll get killed"
"Don't want no one hurt and no blood spilled"
Our tents got tossed all over that hill

(Chorus)

Dan Rather tells it on the evening news
'bout those conservation campers with the bulldozer blues
The oil men were illegal—it's all their fault
And the campers are charging those men with assault

(Chorus)

We got ourselves together up in Oregon Way
Taking on the Forest Service, U.S. of A.
Trying to stop a timber sale
And 44 of us ended up in jail

(Chorus)

Some folks got covered up with dirt
Some got cuffed, and some got hurt
Some had it easy, and some had some luck
And one got hit by a pick-up truck

(Chorus)

The fight against the dozers never really ends
We stood up to the dozers, and we'll do it again
The judge stopped the road up Bald Mountain Way
But, we'll block those dozers again someday

(Chorus)

Back in the Day

Howie Wolke

Five inebriated young men crawled into their sleeping bags under the stars next to a huge volcanic crater in northern Mexico's Pinacate Desert. Somehow, Dave Foreman, Bart Koehler, Ron Kezar, Mike Roselle, and I had managed to get deep into the Pinacate on a series of rough two-track roads in Dave's Volkswagen bus. The VW bus was one of the worst vehicles ever made: massively under-powered, prone to breakdowns, and guaranteed to need an engine rebuild every 60,000 miles. On Dave's van the starter was broken, so each attempt at locomotion required a four-man push start, with Dave getting the cush job of popping the clutch.

We had gone south in April of 1980 to drink beer, eat Mexican food, and explore this wild chunk of Sonoran Desert. It has been reported that the idea of Earth First! materialized as the five of us were descending Pinacate Peak, but that's not accurate. In the Pinacate, we discussed a variety of subjects including the potential collapse of civilization and our love lives (we were in favor of both). But starting a new wilderness group was not deliberated.

Actually, the idea for Earth First! came about after the Pinacate when Dave, Roselle, and I were crossing New Mexico in the VW bus headed toward Albuquerque to eat Dave's mom's home-cooked chicken-fried steak. And the real impetus for the Earth First! founding was the conservation movement's recent failure to defend millions of roadless acres from bulldozers and chainsaws in a 1978-1979 process called RARE II, the Forest Service's second nationwide Roadless Area Review and Evaluation.

You see, in RARE II the Forest Service recommended just 15 million out of 80 million roadless acres for potential Wilderness designation. Much of the remaining acreage would be opened to various multiple (ab)uses including roadbuilding, logging, mining, oil drilling, over-grazing, and off-road vehicles. The Forest Service got away with this travesty largely because the conservation movement didn't push for much wilderness. Instead of advocating wilderness protections for most of the roadless lands, it had recommended less than half of the roadless acreage for Wilderness designation which made it easy for the Forest Service to recommend so little. Led by a small cadre of Washington, D.C., Sierra Club and Wilderness Society lobbyists, the disastrous strategy was meant to look "reasonable" and avoid challenging the Carter Administration. When the appeasement strategy was devised in 1978, Dave still worked for The Wilderness Society (TWS) and he played a limited role in devising the strategy. As the Wyoming Friends of the Earth rep in Wyoming, I was against it from the start, appalled at what the big greens were willing to give up. By the time we got to the Mexican desert, Dave had renounced the strategy of appeasement and resigned from TWS.

RARE II was the grandiose defeat of modern conservation, and it was the major factor in the founding of Earth First!, so let's set the record straight. EF! was not the result of us reading *The Monkey Wrench Gang*, although we were big fans of Edward Abbey's various literary voyages. Nor was the anti-environmental extremism of the Reagan/James Watt years responsible; in fact, in April of 1980, we never dreamed that Americans would soon elect as president a retired grade-B movie actor with limited intellect. Nor did we wish to turn the conservation movement to the political left. No, regardless of what you've heard, Earth First! was incepted as an answer to the RARE II disaster.

As we wobbled in strong crosswinds through New Mexico in Dave's pathetic VW bus hell-bound for fried steak, Dave and I began to discuss the "wimpy" conservation movement. Pretty soon we were ranting and raving. We were angry young men, lubricated by cheap beer, yet possessing a clarity of vision for big wilderness that was clearly lacking in our movement. Dave and I were devising a national system of "ecological preserves" based upon the Bailey-Kuchler "Eco-Regions of the U.S." map, which ironically, had been distributed with the Forest Service's RARE II Final EIS. Soon, we decided to start a new group that would be the no-compromise cutting edge of the wilderness movement. It was an empty niche that needed to be filled. Suddenly, Dave blurted out the words "Earth First" and we had a name. I suggested a green fist in a circle; Roselle quickly drew this, and we had a logo. Within a few weeks, another TWS refugee named Susan Morgan was on board, helping among other things to produce our early newsletters. That's really how Earth First! got started.

Dave and Howie © Dave Foreman Collection
Taking the blessed sacrament in an Albuquerque bar in 2004

Bart Koehler, Ron Kezar, Dave, Mike Roselle © Howie Wolke
An adventure in Pinacate before EF! founding, 1979

For Dave and me, it ended a decade later as urban leftist anarchist social justice activists gained influence, and wilderness was not their priority. In 1990, both Dave and I resigned from Earth First!. I do not know what the latter-day EF! is up to now.

I first met Dave in 1976 through his fellow TWS rep Bart Koehler, when Bart and I were doing field inventories of Wyoming national forest roadless areas. Dave had come north to join our field work, and on one of those jaunts, I remember him being so enthralled with the expansive Absaroka Range alpine tundra that Bart and I could barely get him to descend to camp before dark. "We don't have anything like this in New Mexico," said Dave, with absolute wonder and fascination.

In October 1980, I hitchhiked from Jackson Hole to Albuquerque, where I met Dave for a backpacking trip through his favorite area, the Aldo Leopold and Gila Wildernesses. My old broken-down pickup wouldn't have made it, so I traveled by thumb. Once in the wilds, Dave expected to find water at several springs and small creeks along our route. Dave expected wrong. There were a couple of thirsty nights, but we didn't succumb to renal failure, and overall, it was a great trip. Over the years, when my guiding career periodically took me south to the Gila, I always thought of Dave.

We did some other epic backpack treks, including a ten-day 120-mile walk across the vast South Absaroka wildland in September of '79, starting in Yellowstone and ending up near Dubois, Wyoming. Ron Kezar was with us, and we were all pretty lean and mean in those days. I even have a photo of Dave in all his naked glory standing and flexing atop 12,156-foot Younts Peak, the highest point in the Teton Wilderness.

One aspect of the conservation movement that frustrated both Dave and me was its passive acceptance of agency guidelines for what constitutes a roadless area. It was nearly impossible to develop a good Wilderness proposal for roadless areas that were incompletely mapped. The problem was that each federal agency had its own criteria, and their inventories ended where jurisdictions collided. Therefore, many roadless areas that were large and unbroken on the ground, were hopelessly subdivided on agency maps, masking the true extent of the wildland. For example, in many areas of the West, official Forest Service "roadless areas" end at the national forest boundary while the actual wildland continues down into BLM-administered terrain. But you'd never know it from agency inventories. In addition, both agencies notoriously excluded valuable roadless lands from inventories in order to facilitate potential timber sales or other forms of resource extraction.

In 1936, conservationist Bob Marshall completed the first-ever inventory of large roadless areas in the lower 48 states. He mapped what was roadless on the ground, regardless of agency jurisdiction or land ownership patterns. As previously noted, ensuing agency roadless inventories were shabby and incomplete. Since a comprehensive inventory of big roadless areas hadn't been attempted since 1936, in the mid-'80s Dave and I began to work on *The Big Outside: A Descriptive Inventory of the Big Wilderness Areas of the United States* (latest edition Harmony Books, 1991). *The Big Outside* was Dave's idea, but I enthusiastically agreed for us to join forces as co-authors. Although I am still frustrated at the conservation movement's failure to promote wilderness based upon what is actually on the ground instead of agency boundaries, I am proud of *The Big Outside* as a guide to what the conservation movement should be pushing to protect.

First and foremost, Dave Foreman was a visionary who tirelessly worked for the wilds. He was one of the first to promote the idea of re-wilding. Dave's work ethic bordered on fanatical, or perhaps "obsessive" is a better word. He never shrank from the conviction that human overpopulation was the fundamental cause of nearly all environmental problems—I'm talking eight billion and counting. Nor did he back down from criticizing those in the conservation movement who were weak, even though he always thought—even during our Earth First! days—that the "big greens" were necessary; they just needed to be tougher.

Put simply, the Earth and its wild creatures and habitats need more Dave Foremans, now, more than ever.

Howie Wolke is a retired wilderness guide/outfitter who, during a 41-year career, led over 500 multi-day wilderness backpack treks from northern Alaska to Mexico, including a wide variety of areas throughout the American West. He has encountered well over a hundred grizzlies in the wilds and believes that the Greater Yellowstone Ecosystem is the center of the universe. Howie has worked to protect wilderness and wildlife habitats mostly in the northern U.S. Rockies since 1975, including nearly twenty years as a board director for Wilderness Watch. He has published many articles and two books on the vanishing American Wilderness, *Wilderness On the Rocks* and *The Big Outside*, which was co-authored with Dave Foreman. He has co-founded several wilderness organizations and still believes that all of the earth's remaining wildlands should be protected. As did Dave, Howie also frequently notes that human overpopulation is the most fundamental threat to life on earth. He still goes backpacking (without clients) and also enjoys canoeing, backcountry skiing, whitewater rafting, hunting, wildlife viewing, and birdwatching. He and his wife Marilyn Olsen and their dog Rio live in the foothills of the Gallatin Range in southern Montana, just a few miles from Yellowstone National Park.

Dave and Katie Lee appearing together at
The Abbey Theater in Durango © Dave Foreman Collection

He Changed the Course of My Life

Brad Meiklejohn

Dave Foreman changed the course of conservation. He also changed the course of my life.

I first came upon Dave's ideas in the 1980s while I was working as an avalanche forecaster in Utah. I was introduced to Dave at a talk by Ed Abbey and ended up giving Ed and Dave a ride to the airport. Finally, here were two no-bullshit guys who were making sense. When I departed the avalanche scene, giving up on the recreation rat race, I knew I wanted to put Dave's big ideas into play.

Dave forced us to think BIG. In the 1980s, conservation was concerned with saving the pieces, a whack-a-mole enterprise doomed to failure. Dave drew big, bold lines on the map to capture whole landscapes. His ideas seemed radical at the time, but only because our thinking was too small.

Dave was no radical. He sat squarely in the middle of American conservation tradition, extending the thinking of all the great conservation legends, including Leopold, Hornaday, Muir, Murie, and Brower. Dave knew conservation history and his place in it.

He succeeded in ways big and small. Dave is an unrecognized founder of conservation biology as a practice, which now guides protection and restoration efforts everywhere. Because of Dave, the concept of "big, wild, and connected" is mainstream conservation practice worldwide.

Dave was influential on Doug Tompkins' work that has protected 10 million acres in South America. He inspired me to take down dams, build wildlife highway crossings, and protect as much of Alaska as I could buy.

Dave Foreman lives on in all the world's wildness. Long live Dave Foreman!

Brad Meiklejohn is Senior Alaska Director for The Conservation Fund, where he has worked since 1994. He has directed conservation projects protecting over 300,000 acres of wild land in Alaska, New Hampshire, and Nevada. He is a conservationist, birder, and wilderness explorer who has completed packraft expeditions on 6 continents. Brad served as Associate Director for the Utah Avalanche Center during the 1980s and as President of the Patagonia Land Trust. He is a past board director of The Murie Center and the Alaska Avalanche School.

Alaskan conservationist Brad Meiklejohn lives where he could apply Dave's admonition to "Think Big." An avid outdoorsman, he has traveled and worked in some of the country's wildest landscapes, and he has practiced big, wild, and connected in his campaigns to preserve wild Alaska with remarkable results.

DAVE FOREMAN ABSOLUTELY PUT THE EARTH FIRST

Captain Paul Watson

A left-wing, radically independent Republican who took to the stage like a charismatic ecological evangelical preacher, one of the best public speakers I have ever heard, an astute environmental tactician infused with the courage of a dozen mountain lions.

To me, Dave Foreman, with the looks of a mountain man and the heart of a lion, was first and foremost a natural leader. He co-founded the most famous radical land-based environmental movement on the planet, and his message manifested itself in actions across continents.

Earth First! activists were fiercely fired up by his charisma, his oratory, his writing, and most of all his inventive tactics and keen insight for media.

It was my great honor to have him as a close friend, to work with him, and to watch him in action. We were both inspired by Ed Abbey, and we both were committed to the defense of this beautiful planet, its wondrous wilderness, wildness, and diversity. I was introduced to Dave over 30 years ago by the late, great Edward Abby.

The last time I met with Dave was in 2019 at Lavinia Currier's ranch in Colorado for a sit-down conversation moderated by Mary-Charlotte Domandi for the *Santa Fe New Mexican* podcast. We took a hike together in the mountains where we spent some time observing a colony of ants and sharing our admiration for the ecological importance of all species of ants and other tiny engineers of spaceship Earth.

When the Earth First! message became diluted by the demands of political correctness that insisted on human social justice issues as being more important than the planet, Dave did not fight them. I remember him saying, "When you live in a mansion like Rockefeller, you're going to fight the invaders, but if you live in an Apache Wikiup well, when the vermin move in, you simply move on."

And he did, coining the word Rewilding and founding The Rewilding Institute as he continued to be a strong and passionate force for conservation.

Dave Foreman was the face of radical environmental activism for decades and his field guide to monkeywrenching fell into the eager hands of many passionate nature defenders who became quite skilled at monkeywrenching the weapons and tools of mass ecological destruction.

He forged a reputation for outspoken activism that has been an inspiration for tens of thousands of people.

I can still see and hear him leading a chorus of wolf howls to a pack of Earth-First!ers as a rallying cry for an effective and enduring global movement.

In passing, he moves from incredible activist to an enduring legend.

Long may the wolves howl in memory of this great man.

Captain Paul Watson is a marine wildlife conservation and environmental activist. Watson was one of the founding members and directors of Greenpeace. In 1977, he left Greenpeace and founded the Sea Shepherd Conservation Society. A renowned speaker, accomplished author, master mariner, and lifelong environmentalist, Captain Watson has been awarded many honors for his dedication to the oceans and to the planet.

Among many commendations for his work, he received the Genesis Award for Lifetime Achievement in 1998, was named one of the Top 20 Environmental Heroes of the 20th Century by *Time Magazine* in 2000, and was inducted into the U.S. Animal Rights Hall of Fame in Washington, D.C., in 2002. He was also awarded the Amazon Peace Prize by the president of Ecuador in 2007. In 2012, Captain Watson became only the second person, after Captain Jacques Cousteau, to be awarded the Jules Verne Award, dedicated to environmentalists and adventurers. In 2022, Captain Paul Watson continues his fight for marine wildlife conservation with the new Captain Paul Watson Foundation.

Dave was so proud when Captain Paul would visit him in Albuquerque, big boat and all, and park where people could see who this long-time friend was! They shared an uncompromised dedication to the defense of the natural world. Both risked everything and inspired conservationists and the general public alike.

Muses Come in all Shapes – for Dave

Gary Lawless

you have to feel it in your heart
put your heart on the
line and say
no, no.
you stand in front of the machine.
you chain yourself to the tree, the gate.
you bid on leases.
you go to court.
you go to jail.
your heart tells you
what to do.
you stand between the destroyers,
and the not to be destroyed.
you stand
and your heart sings
with the wild.

Stump Sacred

Gary Lawless

Every stump is sacred.
Every stump a saint.
Every silted river a church to which
the pilgrim salmon return.
Every breath of wind a love song.
We worship in wetlands,
bow to the fern, the rock,
the holy salamander,
the blood of sweet water,
the body of moss.

Gary Lawless is a poet, bioregional advocate, and co-founder of Gulf of Maine Books in Brunswick, Maine. He and his wife Beth Leonard care-take the old farm of Henry Beston and Elizabeth Coatsworth (both acclaimed authors of the mid-20th century), near Damariscotta Lake.

Gary's score of poetry collections includes *Poems for the Wild Earth* and *Caribou Planet.* His newest book of poems is *How the Stones Came to Venice*, and his online poetry blog is http://mygrations.blogspot.com.

Dave Foreman © Brad Richards, Dave Foreman Collection
Firing up an Earth First! Gathering

Dave Foreman: American

Susan Zakin

You know, when I went back to Washington, D.C., to be a lobbyist in the mid-seventies, a U.S. senator put his arm around my shoulder and said, "You know, Dave, we can work with you. You're reasonable. You know how to compromise and consider other interest groups." I was told to put my heart in a safe deposit box and replace my brain with a pocket calculator, to not get emotional. That would harm my argument. I'd ruin my credibility....

But, goddammit, I am emotional! I am passionate. I'm angry. I feel something. I'm not some New Age automaton, some goddamn computer, a pocket calculator. I don't have silicon chips up here. I'm flesh and blood. The winds fill my lungs, the mountains make my bones, the oceans run through my veins. I'm an animal and I'll never be anything but an animal. When a chainsaw rips into a two-thousand-year-old redwood tree, it's ripping into my guts. When a bulldozer plows through a virgin hillside, it's plowing through my side, and when a bullet knocks down a grizzly bear or a wolf, it's going through my heart....

– *Coyotes and Town Dogs*

The last time I saw Dave Foreman it was in the Algonquin Hotel. If that seems an odd venue for a man who described himself as "a hick horseshoer who thinks he's a bronc rider," it wasn't half as odd as the Beaux Arts pile where he and I and Rick Bass were sleeping that night: the New York Yacht Club, an upper crust enclave so steeped in what passes for aristocracy in the U.S. that its members balked at including a photograph of Ted Turner on the wall after the bad boy from Atlanta sailed to victory in the 1977 America's Cup.

Turner wasn't their sort. Neither were we, but Ted Roosevelt IV, an investment banker trying to stop the depredations of latter-day Republicans, had invited us to speak at a roundtable there. Hell, it was a free trip to New York. The invitation was also a mark of just how far a New Mexico military brat had traveled, and despite his protestations, how comfortably he fit in with his generation's significant political figures.

Foreman, who died September 19, 2022, was cast in the same mold as Turner: brilliant, charismatic, and above all, just crazy enough to believe he was right even when more conventional people told him he couldn't be. It is not too much to say that the self-proclaimed hick horseshoer was the environmental movement's Martin Luther King, Bobby Kennedy, and Bob Dylan rolled into one. His critics would note a touch of Elmer Gantry.

I have always believed that the environmental movement is a phenomenon of the American West, and Foreman's roots in the West ran deep. A fourth-generation New Mexican, his family had crossed the frontier in Conestoga wagons. He had the Westerner's gift for flouting convention, or perhaps just being oblivious to it. For him, that meant leaving his job as The Wilderness Society's top Washington, D.C., lobbyist and, along with the other members of the environmental Round Table, latter-day knights-errant in cowboy boots Bart Koehler, Mike Roselle (less cowboy than yippie), Louisa Willcox, Susan Morgan, Ron Kezar, and Howie Wolke, embarking on a guerrilla theater cum revolution-for-the-hell-of-it road show called Earth First!.

Like the Algonquin's Round Table, which started when his fellow writers suckered Wolcott into a lunch where they proceeded to roast him for his braggodocio, Earth First! began with a stunt. In 1981, the founders unfurled a 300-foot strip of black plastic, a "crack" down the face of Glen Canyon Dam in Utah, the symbol of the worst excesses of industrializing the frontier. The guerrilla theater had a lighthearted tone, but the ideas behind Earth First! were serious. Foreman and the other Earth First! founders—the best and brightest of their generation of environmentalists—understood the magnitude of the extinction crisis before their Washington, D.C., counterparts. They realized that efforts to preserve nature in the U.S., although well-intentioned for their time, weren't based on science, and our parks, forests, and wildlife refuges couldn't keep alive the millions of species threatened with extinction.

Steeped in the new science of conservation biology pioneered by Harvard biologist E.O. Wilson and others, Foreman and the renegades who called themselves Earth First! realized that the world was undergoing its sixth major extinction event and the only one caused by humans. By 1980, scientists were predicting the loss of 15-20 percent of all species by 2000. Thomas Lovejoy wrote in 2013 that these numbers had been close to what actually happened. Now the United Nations estimates that 1 million of the world's plants and animals are in danger of extinction.

Outdoors-people saw animals and plants disappearing before their eyes. For these people, frustrated by the environmental movement's increasing reliance on lawyers rather than visionaries, Earth First!'s message was a resounding one. By 1990, the anarchist group had attracted thousands of followers, from hippied-out misfits to college professors.

All of the founders deserved credit for the group's popularity, but it wouldn't have happened without Foreman's rhetorical skills. When you heard him talk, you experienced birth, life, and death in one long impassioned exhortation, and you were changed. Even if you were a skeptical reporter.

Like many Americans, I grew up with a romantic idea of the American landscape before the closing of the frontier. Foreman offered a vision of rolling back that line, expunging the ugliness of industrialization and its inhumanness. The idea of a lost Eden is out of style now, but the vision remains moving for many of us, even if only as an aesthetic, and it is profoundly American.

In the late 1980s, I was looking for a way to write a history of the environmental movement, and I had a penchant for rebelliousness myself. With the help of David Stanford, an editor at Viking, I approached Foreman with the idea of a book that would combine the history of the conservation movement with the gonzo tales of Earth First!. Against the advice of his wife, Nancy Morton, who wanted him to concentrate on finishing his own account (later published as *Confessions of an Eco-Warrior*) Dave agreed to work with me. I immersed myself in the facts of his life, traveling to the places he had lived, from Zuni, New Mexico, where he had worked in a Head Start program and steeped himself in Zuni ritual, to Blythe, California, where I unearthed a high school yearbook with the obligatory dorky headshot. I interviewed his mother and sister, and hit the library, looking up his influences, including the frontier church that had formed his galvanizing speaking style. In turn, he educated me on the history of the conservation movement, which I began to see as a window to what our current president calls "the soul of America." We were, and continue to be, a culture shaped by the frontier. For good or ill. If anyone doubts this, they have only to look at the self-styled "patriots" who have displaced environmentalists as the radicals of our time.

Paradoxically, I found that Foreman, whose onstage rhetorical skills rivaled Jesse Jackson's, was rather shy in private. A few weeks into my research, I called him. Knowing he was rabidly atheistic, I hesitantly asked about the Church of Christ, the Protestant denomination whose preachers espoused a rugged individualism that brought Westerners into direct relation with God, never mind about the church bureaucracy. The Church of Christ flourished on the frontier, attracting throngs to billowing tents with its quasi-libertarian ethos.

Fearing that I was about to blow the prospect of the book, along with any liking he might have for me, I asked him if the anarchistic makeup of Earth First! mirrored that of the church.

He burst out laughing. "I've been waiting ten years for someone to ask me that question," he said. We were off and running. For the next year, I traveled around, talking to Earth-First!ers around the country, groups of people whose causes and tactics mirrored their region of the U.S., and who operated fairly independently—anarchists, right?—but whose values had been articulated by Foreman and the others.

The people of Earth First! had the misfortune to be Cassandras. As far back as 1981, they proposed setting aside 44 wilderness areas of 1 million acres each, carefully chosen ecosystems that would serve as biological preserves. It sounded crazy then, 44 million acres out of the 1.9 billion that make up the United States. As it turns out, the Earth First! proposal was moderate, if you were talking scientific reality. In 2016, Harvard's E.O. Wilson, whose work had inspired them at the outset, proposed setting aside half the earth as biological preserves.

The men and women of Earth First! were too far ahead of their time to be taken seriously by politicians, especially with an anti-environmental backlash in full swing. And Earth First!'s leaders were too easily seduced by the media attention they received for their most controversial behavior. Inspired by Edward Abbey's novel *The Monkey Wrench Gang*, Earth First!

went beyond respectable tactics of non-violent passive resistance. While some Earth-First!ers chained themselves to fences, stood in front of bulldozers, and blockaded logging roads, others hammered large nails into trees slated for logging, then called the media to say they'd done it, slowing and sometimes stopping timber sales. Still others poured sand in bulldozer gas tanks, clipped powerlines with cutting torches, and burned billboards. No doubt there were other incidents of what Abbey had called ecosabotage or *nachtwerk*, inspired by the 19th-century Luddites who broke into textile factories to destroy looms that were putting them out of jobs. These extra-legal activities not only got the attention of the media; eventually, they attracted the FBI's notice.

Dave Foreman had once been a skinny, sensitive, 98-pound weakling kid who devoured books about animals. "He wouldn't step on a spider," his mother Lorane told me. By 1991, *Outside* magazine was referring to him as "arguably the most dangerous environmentalist in America."

Was Foreman dangerous because of his actions or his ideas? I'd venture to say that it was Foreman's ideas, combined with the power of his speaking style, that landed him in a Prescott, Arizona, courtroom with four co-defendants after an FBI sting. The case was eventually plea bargained, and the prodigal Foreman returned to the tribe from which he had distanced himself, serving on the board of the Sierra Club until a disagreement over immigration resulted in his ouster, starting The Wildlands Project, an organization dedicated to creating biological reserves minus the monkeywrenching, and co-founding the New Mexico Wilderness Alliance with his wife Nancy.

The later years were more peaceful. He spent time with scientists like Michael Soulé, the founder of the Society for Conservation Biology, and self-made men like himself: Doug Tompkins, the co-founder of Esprit clothing, who had devoted his fortune to protecting the Alerce forest in Chile, and Yvon Chouinard, the climber, outdoorsman, and founder of Patagonia, who recently gave his billion-dollar company to a conservation trust.

Serious people, all of them. Major players. I imagine Dave asked himself at the end of his life whether he had made a difference. No single individual can stop population growth, and that remains the inexorable killer of species. Foreman, like Ed Abbey before him, hit a wall intellectually on this question.

But I know that Dave Foreman, directly and indirectly, saved the beauty of the world. Some of it, at least. And I know, too, that as befits a man with larger-than-life rhetorical gifts, he changed the conversation. Extinction still doesn't get the attention that climate change does, even though the two operate synergistically and scientists say they are equal threats to the survival of the planet. But the death of all that lives around us, and in some fundamental sense, makes our lives worth living, is no longer ignored.

The politics have changed, too, albeit slowly. Without Earth First!, it's unlikely that there would be the Center for Biological Diversity. Starting with $5,000 and two guys in a New Mexico ranch house using government documents for toilet paper, the Center now has staff lawyers, a $14 million a year budget, and an 80 percent courtroom win rate. It seems equally unlikely that the international civil disobedience group Extinction Rebellion would exist if it hadn't been for Earth First!.

There will be no headstone for Dave Foreman. Like Edward Abbey, he preferred to have his corporeal self left in nature, food for the living things he fought so hard to keep with us. If he had one, the inscription, perhaps, could simply read: *Dave Foreman, American.*

Dave Foreman changed the way we thought about our country and about nature. It's not turning back the frontier and restoring Eden, but it's still the best we have.

Known for her forthrightness, lyricism, and humor, Susan Zakin is one of America's most respected environmental writers. A graduate of Columbia University's Graduate School of Journalism, Zakin's articles and essays have appeared in *Vogue*, *Salon*, *The New York Times*, *Orion*, and many other publications. She is the author of *Coyotes and Town Dogs: Earth First! and the Environmental Movement*, which established her as a trenchant, irreverent commentator on U.S. environmental politics. After covering the anti-environmental backlash in Washington, D.C., as a magazine columnist and syndicated newspaper columnist, in 2001, she lived in Madagascar as the Senior John Heinz Fellow in Environmental Reporting. In 2020, she founded *Journal of the Plague Year*, an online magazine of journalism and literary writing that is a response to the Balkanization that's impoverished both journalism and creative nonfiction. The Journal, which she edits, has been compared to *The Village Voice* in its heyday. This tribute to Dave was first published in *Journal of the Plague Year*. www.journaloftheplagueyear.ink.

Moving the Needle

Andy Kerr

"Kerr. Dave Foreman. I'm coming to Oregon. Do you want me to damn you or praise you? Whatever you think best."

So began a telephone call I received from Dave Foreman in 1983. Dave was coming to attempt to stop the infamous Bald Mountain Road, a Forest Service project to sever the North Kalmiopsis wildlands in southwest Oregon so the area could never be added to the existing Kalmiopsis Wilderness.

A Congressional Battle Between Good and Evil

In early 1978, after a political pissing match of epic proportions, US Senator Mark Hatfield (R-OR) and Rep. Jim Weaver (D-4th OR) agreed to expand the then 78,850-acre Kalmiopsis Wilderness—first designated a "Wild Area" by the Forest Service in 1946 and made a wilderness by Congress in 1964—by ~92,000 acres. Actually, Weaver never agreed. Hatfield was far more powerful, and when there is a difference between the House of Representatives and the Senate, often they split the difference. Not in this case.

Hatfield's first legislation called for expanding the Kalmiopsis by 134,000 acres, as did Weaver's first bill. However, Weaver also initially called for the designation of another 136,000 acres as a wilderness study area, which would set the area on a path toward eventual inclusion in the Kalmiopsis Wilderness. However, by the time the House voted on Weaver's proposal, the entire 270,000 acres would be slated for wilderness designation. Offended that Weaver would expand his Kalmiopsis proposal, in his pique and with his power, Hatfield dialed back his own original 134,000-acre Kalmiopsis addition by 51,600 acres to 82,400 acres.

Hatfield, if not bought and sold by Big Timber, was so leased and rented. While both ends of the Kalmiopsis were wild and wonderful, the South Kalmiopsis didn't have much commercial timber, being mainly a serpentine landscape. However, the North Kalmiopsis had lots of virgin old-growth forests.

A conference committee of representatives and senators convened to resolve the differences between the two bills. Going in, most thought that Weaver and Hatfield would resolve their 187,600-acre difference by reverting to the common 134,000 acres of Kalmiopsis additions they had both originally supported. No such luck. After a lot of pissing, moaning, bitching, and whining all around, Weaver and Hatfield grudgingly agreed on a 92,000-acre addition (in the end, a classic splitting the difference almost evenly, though Hatfield came out 1,800 acres better than Weaver). The new boundary was drawn along the east-west ridge of Bald Mountain that separated the mainstem Illinois River to the south and the Silver Creek watershed to the north.

Coincidentally, watching Hatfield act out in the conference committee that day was a lobbyist from The Wilderness Society by the name of Dave Foreman.

The House committee staff knew the area better than their Senate counterparts, so the northern boundary of this new Wilderness addition was actually drawn not quite on the hydrological divide but rather just northward and downslope enough to—because of the hellishly steep terrain—preclude the planned Bald Mountain Road, which the Forest Service had devised to open the area to clearcut liquidation.

Shortly after the bill was signed into law, Hatfield found out he'd been quietly had and even more quietly passed a "rider" to move the boundary and shrink the wilderness to allow the logging road to be built. Additionally, as chair of the Senate Committee on Appropriations, he made sure the Forest Service had all the money it needed to build the Bald Mountain Road, $1,485,000 ($7.1 million in today's money).

This loss of those 102 acres (but who's counting?) of the Kalmiopsis Wilderness arguably resulted in the first skirmish in what would later be known as the Pacific Northwest Forest Wars.

Post-Legislation Confrontations

Litigation, Round 1

In 1979, just a year after the congressional Kalmiopsis calamity, the Forest Service approved the Bald Mountain Road and the multiple timber sales it would allow. In 1982, the Sierra Club and the organization now known as Oregon Wild (then the Oregon Wilderness Coalition [OWC]) brought suit in federal court to stop the Bald Mountain Road. Since the Club was paying the lawyer, it was calling the shots, and as an OWC staffer, I begged and cajoled the Sierra Club on several issues to no avail. For political reasons in Congress, the Sierra Club lawsuit intentionally chose not to cite as precedent a very successful lawsuit brought by the State of California against the Forest Service that overturned the agency's second Roadless Area Review and Evaluation (RARE II) in that state. Rather, the legal complaint was a standard challenge under the National Environmental Policy Act. While OWC disagreed with this strategy, it had no money for its own lawyer to bring the very likely winning claim. U.S. District Court Judge Helen Frye found for the Forest Service.

Construction began on the Bald Mountain Road but was soon shut down by winter.

Protest

Things were looking bad for the North Kalmiopsis. There was no legislative option, and litigation had failed. President Jimmy Carter's Administration had offered the RARE II process during hearings on what would become the Endangered American Wilderness Act, which had expanded (somewhat) the Kalmiopsis Wilderness. The Carter Administration was rolled by its own Forest Service, and when the RARE II dust had settled, the agency was recommending, out of 66 million roadless acres reviewed (the agency refused to inventory a lot of qualifying land), only 15 million acres for wilderness (mainly rock and ice) and another 11 million acres for additional review later. Thirty-six million acres of roadless areas, including the North Kalmiopsis, were to be sacrificed to development and exploitation.

The disaster that was RARE II was a radicalizing event for the four guys—including one Dave Foreman—who founded Earth First!. Playing nice with a supposedly sympathetic administration was not cutting it. As there were no options in the arenas of legislation or litigation, it was time for the arena of protest. The new Earth First! was looking for trouble and found plenty in Josephine County, Oregon.

In the spring of 1983, local citizens—aided by the outside agitators from Earth First!—commenced a string of blockades and protests designed to delay the bulldozers and chainsaws from defiling Bald Mountain. First, and longest, on the scene was another Earth First! founder, one Mike Roselle. Roselle, partly by using some walking around money spent mostly on beer, but mostly by using inspiration, perspiration, and organization, convened a rag-tag coalition of locals and outsiders who flocked to the cause (some of whom went on to have distinguished careers in mainstream conservation) to do what they could to stop the Forest Service. Roselle was the glue that held the effort together. By July 1983, there had been seven blockades with 47 people getting arrested. The story of the protests, including Earth First!'s role, is beautifully and movingly told in Susan Zakin's book, *Coyotes and Town Dogs: Earth First! and the Environmental Movement.*

Here I shall only recount the incident in which Dave Foreman was dragged under the road contractor's pickup for 103 yards (but who's counting?). This account is from *The Earth First! Reader: Ten Years of Radical Environmentalism*:

> *Then on May 12, Dave Willis [later the catalyst for the Cascade-Siskiyou National Monument] and Dave Foreman set up a roadblock on the access road 10 miles from the construction area to stop the [road contractor] Plumly workers on their way to work. With their support team, they pulled a downed tree into the road in front of themselves, because, as Foreman said, "I don't want to be a hood ornament on a Plumly truck."*
>
> *At 6 AM, a sheriff's deputy arrived and asked them to move. They refused. The deputy then winched the log out of the way and parked 50 feet in front of them. Wills, missing both hands and feet from frostbite, was in his wheelchair. At 6:15, the Plumly sixpac pickup carrying five workers arrived and drove around the deputy's vehicle. The workers tried to pass Willis on the inside of the road cut, but Foreman stepped over and blocked their path. They then drove to the outside of the road bend. Foreman stepped back in place.*
>
> *For a moment, the blockaders faced off the truck. Then it shot forward, hitting Foreman in the chest and knocking him back five feet. Again, truck*

> *and man faced off. The truck pushed against Foreman. He pushed back. Les Moore, the driver, accelerated. Foreman had to backpedal to keep from being run over. He finally lost his balance and went down. He held on to the bumper for a few seconds and the truck finally stopped... after having pushed him a distance later measured as 103 yards.*
>
> *The five construction workers lept out of the truck and surrounded Foreman, who was lying half under it. "You dirty communist bastard," yelled Les Moore. "Why don't you go back to Russia where you came from?"*
>
> *"But, Les," Foreman replied, "I'm a registered Republican."*

The deputy then arrested Foreman for disorderly conduct and took him to the Josephine County jail in Grants Pass. Foreman made bail that afternoon. The Sheriff's Office and the Forest Service maintained that no assault occurred, merely that Foreman stepped in front of the moving truck that immediately stopped. That's not what a United Press International reporter wrote from the scene or what two local television crews had filmed.

Litigation, Round 2

In late 1982, the US 9th Circuit Court of Appeals had upheld the district court ruling in California against the Forest Service. By this time, the Oregon Wilderness Coalition had renamed itself the Oregon Natural Resources Council (ONRC) on its way to becoming Oregon Wild. Protests are newsworthy. People were calling ONRC and asking what they could do. I suggested they send us some money so we can sue the Forest Service again the right way. Enough did send money. Not enough for us to actually pay for an attorney, but enough to cover ONRC's costs. Most fortunately, a recent University of Oregon School of Law graduate had hung his shingle in Roseburg, Oregon, which billed itself as the "timber capital of the world." Doing divorce cases wasn't why Neil Kagan went to law school, but saving nature was. Kagan jumped at the chance to litigate again the matter of the Bald Mountain Road—this time citing slam-dunk precedent.

ONRC, unlike the Sierra Club, feared nature's backlash more than any congressional backlash. In honor of Earth First!'s unconventional contribution to saving the North Kalmiopsis from the dagger that was the Bald Mountain

Road, Kagan listed Earth First! as the lead plaintiff in the case, along with ONRC and seven individuals.

Kagan won the case. Big time. Judge James Redden enjoined further construction of the road and any associated timber sales. For down and dirty on the legal machinations, I highly recommend Kagan's law review article, "Wilderness, Luck and Love: A Memoir and a Tribute." It reads like no other law review article you've ever read. It is the story of Kagan's role in litigating to protect Forest Service roadless areas and his love of both nature and the law, intertwined with his love for his wife Betty Reed, who left us far too soon. Though it was the second litigation that eventually saved the day, it was direct, sometimes illegal—but always moral—acts of citizens who ran to the noise of the bulldozers and chainsaws that made the difference.

Earth First!'s role in total—not just Foreman's ride under a logging crummy—in stopping, along with locals, is one for the history books.

The Long View/Fight

The North Kalmiopsis wildlands, for which Dave Foreman nearly lost his life trying to save from the bulldozer and the chainsaw, are still not, some four decades later, fully protected for the benefit of this and future generations. The remaining roadless wildlands have not yet been added to the Kalmiopsis Wilderness, but much of the roadless area is somewhat administratively protected as a Forest Service Inventoried Roadless Area. Some of the lands have received wild and scenic river status and more is in the offing. Perhaps its mature and old-growth forests will be administratively protected by the Biden Administration.

Sometimes, it takes a lot of time to save a piece of nature. Dave Foreman knew this. Dave also knew that—given the rate of the human assault on nature—nature doesn't have the luxury of time.

In my view, Dave Foreman's greatest contributions to saving the wild were:

- getting conservationists, and then society to think bigger;
- invoking science to save wilderness when the science of its values was still emerging; and
- having a large and secure ego to let other egos take credit and run with ideas he first popularized.

The Overton Window

I didn't know it at the time, and probably neither did Dave, but Dave's fundamental course was trying to move what the socio-political chattering class now calls the Overton Window.

The Overton Window is the thinking of Joseph P. Overton of the Mackinac Center for Public Policy, a conservative think tank. According to *Wikipedia*, "The Overton Window is the range of policies politically acceptable to the mainstream population at a given time. It is also known as the window of discourse." When Dave started his conservation career, wilderness was within the Overton Window, but generally more because of human recreation than nature conservation. Wilderness also had to be relatively large areas, and generally was more rock and ice than low-elevation forests or desert grasslands.

The Overton Window is not moved by politicians, rather it is moved by think tanks and activists who advocate for policy solutions that start outside the range of public acceptability. As the unpopular, if not previously unspoken, idea moves to become more popular, the Overton Window moves to reflect that, and policy solution is now within the realm of political discussion.

I recall a conversation with Dave that hit home with me. He explained that the public lands conservation movement generally came from the progressive movement, and more on the Republican than Democratic wings. Early 20th-century public lands conservationists like John Muir, Stephen Mather, Horace Albright, Gifford Pinchot, and their like were all white, Republican, and rich. They didn't want to rock the socio-political boat, but rather just change its course A bit. Not turn the boat around—and if any rocking was required—not too much rocking.

"Where would Martin Luther King (Jr.) have been without Malcolm X?" thundered Dave, just to me at that point, but it was a line from a speech that he had or would give many times. The radical Malcolm X did make MLK appear more reasonable in the public arena.

Foreman helped the public lands conservation community think (and act) "outside the box," another metaphor for the limits of public acceptability. Dave taught me that while ecological realities are immutable, political realities are mutable. Only if one has one's idea aperture too small and/ or time horizon too short, does it appear that political realities cannot be changed.

It's the Science, Stupid

Foreman was not a scientist, but early on in his conservation career, he knew—in his gut if not yet his head—if we're to have functioning ecosystems across the landscape (and seascape) over time, at least half of every ecosystem needs to be conserved and, in some cases, restored. Later Foreman came to know this to be the case not only in his gut but in his head. As the discipline of conservation biology emerged, Dave embraced and popularized the science that provided objective evidence for what was previously just his personal testimony.

Today, the conservation buzz is all about "30x30," or conserving 30% of the world's, nation's/state's lands and waters by 2030. Don't tell anyone, but 30x30 is simply an interim goal of doing 50x50, which is where the science points. Yep, 50% by 2050.

Acquiescing, Even Urging, His Colleagues to Steal His Ideas

As Dave helped move nature conservation's Overton Window, he was genuinely pleased when others took credit for his work, credit for either the moving of the political window itself or for taking advantage of the concept/ idea/notion/necessity that the moved Overton Window exposed. More than one chief executive officer of national conservation organizations told Dave to his face that they were embracing "his" idea (of course, without crediting him). Foreman's response was always not "you're welcome," but rather "go for it."

While Foreman did radical things on behalf of nature, in his chest beat the heart of a reactionary deeply opposed to any so-called "progress" that came at the cost to the wild. It is not that he opposed civilization or was misanthropic. Rather, Foreman realized that for there to be fine cigars and exquisite liquors and the many other products of civilization that we enjoy and for our children to inhabit and prosper, the Earth must continue to provide fundamental ecosystem goods and services, not just society providing peripheral economic goods and services.

So, did Dave end up damning or praising me when he came to southwest Oregon? Depending on his audience, both. It worked for me, it worked for him, and most importantly, it worked for nature.

Foreman moved the needle.

Andy Kerr is the Czar of The Larch Company (www.andykerr.net) and is best known for his two decades with the Oregon Wild (then Oregon Natural Resources Council), the organization best known for having brought you the northern spotted owl. Kerr began his conservation career during the Ford Administration. Through 2022, Kerr has been closely involved with the establishment or expansion of 47 Wilderness Areas and 57 Wild and Scenic Rivers, 13 congressionally legislated special management areas, 15 Oregon Scenic Waterways, and one proclaimed national monument (and later expanded). He has testified before congressional committees on several occasions. Kerr authored *Oregon Desert Guide: 70 Hikes* (The Mountaineers Books, 2000) and *Oregon Wild: Endangered Forest Wilderness* (Timber Press, 2004).

Current projects include advocating for additional Wilderness and Wild and Scenic Rivers, achieving the permanent protection and restoration of mature and old-growth forests, facilitating voluntary federal grazing permit buyouts, conserving and restoring the Sagebrush Sea, opposing oil and gas exploitation onshore and offshore, and saving Oregon's Elliott State Forest.

"Moving the Needle" first appeared in Andy Kerr's *Public Lands Blog* (https://www.andykerr.net/kerr-public-lands-blog).

Confessions of an Eco-Warrior

The true ecoterrorists are the planet-despoilers: Those in the Forest Service and the timber industry who are annihilating thousand-year-old forests for paper bags and picnic tables. Ranchers and employees of the Department of Agriculture's Animal Damage Control unit who have exterminated predators ranging from Grizzly Bears and Gray Wolves to common Ravens and Bobcats and continue to slaughter them in their remnant ranges. The calculator-rational engineers and pork-barrel politicians who want to plug every free-flowing river with dams. The thrill-seeking dirt bikers who terrify wildlife and scar delicate watersheds with mindless play. Japanese and Icelandic whalers who are hounding the last great whales to the ends of the Earth, despite international agreements against whaling. The heads of Exxon and other giant oil companies who cut back on safety measures to save a few pennies and thereby cause disasters like the Prince William Sound oil-tanker wreck and the blowout of drilling platforms in the Santa Barbara Channel. Corporate executives whose bottom line is profit and who could not care less about Love Canals, Bhopals, cigarette smoke, acid rain, and unsafe automobiles. Otherworldly "religious leaders" who condemn birth control and encourage the poor in Third World counties to have more children. The list of ecoterrorists is endless—but it does not include the brave and conscientious individuals who are defending threatened wild areas by placing a monkeywrench into the gears of the machine.

– Dave Foreman
Confessions of an Eco-Warrior

How David Foreman Inspired Me and Our Nevada Wilderness Advocacy Community

Karen (Tanner) Boeger

It all began in the late 1970s when this Nevada newbie volunteer Wilderness advocate walked into a Denver seminar room. A Forest Service person was holding forth about the RARE II public process to rate FS roadless areas for their Wilderness attributes. Knowing no one, I stood toward the back of the room thinking about where to sit. Leaning at a "question authority" angle against the back wall were three young men with a somewhat ruffian appearance: flannel-shirted, sleeves rolled up, muscular arms crossed, cowboy booted and hatted, boots casually crossed at ankles. My teacher alarm said, "hmmm, looks like those middle-school-back-of-the-room-looking-for-trouble boys." One of them I later learned was David; already clearly a preach-erman, he asked the speaker an aptly challenging question, which was one I shared, so I promptly tuned in. After the unsatisfactory answer, the three began muttering among themselves, making disparaging remarks about "the process." I edged closer to hear what I could learn—and well, that was that: we met. I got an animated crash course in effective NEPA comments and the energizing power of making a difference for the Wilderness cause. We exchanged contact info and became fast friends as fellow warriors in a small circle of Wilderness advocates throughout the West.

A long winding trail ensued, but the next stop was a small gathering in the late 1970s near Las Vegas, NM, to which the trio had invited me. Another pivotal "buckaroo in training" experience from those early days was my first visit to Washington, DC. I had been selected by Nevada's Sierra Club to carry

Dave and Karen Boeger after receiving their awards from Great Old Broads for Wilderness, 50th Anniversary Wilderness Act gathering, 2014 © Karen Boeger Collection

our bundle of James Watt petitions to join the USA-wide demonstration on the Capitol steps where we delivered our bundles to Congress. David and Bart were there to greet me and provide some lobbying pointers for when I met with my delegation.

In about 1980, I felt honored to receive a surprise invitation from David to what he later called the Round River Rendezvous (RRR), after our hero Aldo Leopold, to be held at the T-Cross Ranch near DuBois, Wyoming. The intent of the gathering was rest and relaxation for hard-working Wilderness compadres, with evening campfire social gatherings, complete with tale-swapping, and a songfest led by cowpoke crooner Bart Koehler, soon to enter EF! history as Johnny Sagebrush. Another purpose appeared to be a therapy session since most invitees were Western state field representatives for The Wilderness Society, who had just resigned or been fired by new Executive Director Bill Turnage. Around the campfire one evening, after a tasty steak dinner grilled by Mike Roselle, "The Kid," the now legendary desert trek origin myth was told, with the proposition that a kick-ass Defense of Mother Earth "dis-organization" should be created. We all said, "Hell yes! Let's DO it!" That gathering itself energized us, the concept of EF! alone giving us a sense of strength in common cause going forward. Thus commenced a relationship with David as mentor, co-conspirator, friend, and so much more over subsequent decades.

David, with the back-up posse of his buckaroo "saddlepal" partners, touched off pivotal sparks in my own activist DNA, augmenting my passionate conviction that there could be no greater legacy in my life than to do what I could to conserve, protect, and restore every piece of existing undeveloped public land with Wilderness characteristics and/or potential to restore those characteristics. We could do that by seeking wilderness designation or other protective categories like WSA, ACEC, NCA, or national monument status for places with wilderness character. We could try to stop threats to wilderness by fighting timber sales and road-building.

David's fire-brand sermons inspired me in those early days of my activism. The tools were his incantations: "Do Something! Never give up! Question authority!" This inspiration bore fruit for me in 1980 when I filed my first two BLM WSA appeals in Nevada against the agency's decision to overlook two significant wilderness areas in their designations. Without any legal experience or having challenged a NEPA decision, I carefully read over all the steps to file an appeal, sent off my hand-written appeal, got called to the IBLA regional office in CA to state my case, and a miracle ensued: I won both appeals! It's hard to adequately describe my astonishment and joy. One determined school teacher stood up to a giant Federal Agency, made her case, and won! Ever since, I have recounted that story to every new young wild warrior who crosses my path, to share the sense that yes, we can make a difference if we take an action and do not give up!

Another key "tool to success" David preached was one he had absorbed from Ed Abbey in his famous quotation: "Do not burn yourselves out … enjoy the land while you can, while it is there…. run the rivers ... and I promise you shall outlive the bastards!" David embraced this admonition by the way he lived his life, not only in the adventures he had and the rivers he ran but also in his sense of childlike joy while doing so, letting loose with wolf howls or the playful call of the tiny chickadee.

When David visited Ely, Nevada, in the mid-80s to inventory a number of Nevada WSAs for potential Wilderness designation, his joy in playful fun was a part of our adventure. Here is one story: After exploring the natural wonders of the Desatoya Mountains (just now finally designated Wilderness by Congress in December 2022!), we decided to camp at Sand Mountain, an iconic formation along the "Loneliest Highway" (Hwy 50), sacred to the local tribes, but sadly now over-run with sand buggies. We had heard stories that at the crest of the mountain, with even the tiniest breeze, the sand would "sing." The moon was full, so of course we had to climb this impressively steep mountain of sand to discover if it would sing to us. At the top, we sat straddling the very spine of the mountain, silently soaking in the moonlit surreal scene, listening for what the mountain might say. To our amazement, we heard a soft shushing sound that kept us spellbound for a while before we jumped up and excitedly went laughing, running, stumbling, tumbling all the way back down to camp. This is a side of David that is rarely seen in public, so resonant with my own. Keeping his senses open to the wonderments that Nature could provide, he enjoyed spontaneous, joyful, childlike behavior when he was outside, as on the "singing mountain," and so did I—a bonding component of our lifetime friendship.

David the preacher cemented our sense of being a righteous army in defense of Mother Earth in his sermons and his example. Beyond our foundational EF! years, David increasingly embraced his more quiet, visionary self, working with noted science visionaries in developing key new concepts such as connectivity and rewilding. These concepts brought public recognition that Wilderness and undeveloped spaces are essential for human quality of life. He made a strong case that they are essential also for the health of the planet, and are the life essentials for all wildlife viability, and for healthy genetic diversity in all species. These aspirational concepts have become foundational pieces added to conservation advocacy and woven into our activism. Expanded conceptions of the health of our planet and all beings are a tremendous legacy. David's lifetime of personal growth, evolving and expanding his conservation brain and producing numerous books along the way, has been a key enabling factor for my own conservation brain expansion and that of many others in our conservation community.

On a near daily basis in my continuing conservation work, there is not a single written or verbal public land health comment I make that has not been influenced by the absorption of David's passion and his visionary essential concepts, including the many avenues we must pursue—and never give up!—in our quest to restore, protect, and conserve the health of our planet and all the creatures that call it home.

Karen (Tanner) Boeger, a retired school teacher, Nevadan "Desert Rat," and volunteer conservation activist for over forty years, is a founding member of Friends of Nevada Wilderness.

She has participated in various stakeholder Advisory Committees for the BLM and has been an advocate for public lands, wildlife, and quiet recreation at both the state and federal levels. In addition to the Friends of Nevada Wilderness Board, Karen currently also serves on the Boards of the Nevada Chapter of Backcountry Hunters and Anglers and the Nevada Wildlife Coalition.

In her words: I was fortunate to grow up at a time when much of the West was still wild and the dominant recreational uses were traditional: hiking, fishing, hunting, and horseback riding, with the addition of an occasional post-WW2 jeep. Within a generation, opportunities for those experiences have vastly diminished. My advocacy work is dedicated to ensuring that my grandchildren and all future generations always have the same public land and wilderness opportunities that I enjoyed.

It's Hard to Imagine a World Without Dave

Shaaron Netherton

I first met Dave at a bus stop in Winnemucca, Nevada. He and Bart were traveling in Dave's old van, and they stopped to pick up Karen Boeger and me. We were going to travel together up to the Malheur Refuge Wilderness Conference. All that Earth First! stuff was totally new to me, a fairly young and green BLM employee. I have to say that trip changed the trajectory of my life in ways I would never have guessed at the time.

Later, living with Bart and Dave in Ely, Nevada, it was clear my life would never be the same. Through them, I met so many good folks at Round River Rendezvous, rafting trips, road shows, trips to Mexico, and more. I miss all those crazy people and look forward to the stories, in person at the June celebration of Dave's life, I hope. While I have stayed very close to Bart over the years, I regret that I didn't keep in touch with Dave as much as I could or should have. I feel so blessed to have talked with him on the Saturday before he passed. I will treasure his final words to me.

– Shaaron (AKA Wildcat Annie)

Shaaron Netherton has served as Executive Director for Friends of Nevada Wilderness since July 2000, becoming the organization's first full-time director. She has built Friends of Nevada Wilderness into a strong, vibrant organization with a string of wilderness legislative successes leading to the protection of over 3 million acres of wilderness. She received her BS degree in Wildlife Management from Humboldt State University. Prior to accepting the ED position, Shaaron was a field manager with the Bureau of Land Management in Prineville, Oregon. She has 22 years of public land management experience in the BLM, with 10 years in Nevada working specifically in the BLM's Wilderness program.

Ode to Dave Foreman

By Uncle Ramon

(Who sent it to Karen Pickett, and asked her to send it to Bron Taylor, who sent it to The Rewilding Institute)

Ding-dong; the beast is dead.
But what a lot of change he led.
Now it's up to us instead.
Ding-dong; the beast is dead.

Others thought they'd have their way
And wilderness all gone away.
But they no longer hold much sway:
The world now knows the price we pay.

So here's a toast from me and you
(To Mike, Howie, Bart and Susan too)
They sure begat a lively crew
Who visualize a world that's new.

Nonetheless, our beast is dead.
"Keep it Wild" is what he pled.
"No compromise" were words he said.
So now it's up to us instead.

(Apologies to Dr. Suess)

Long Conversations Over the Years

Bruce Hamilton

I first knew of Dave Foreman when he was one of the Western field organizers for The Wilderness Society (TWS) in the 1970s. I was a field editor for *High Country News* and covered wilderness and wildlands issues throughout the West, and later was Northern Plains/Northern Rockies Regional Representative for the Sierra Club. I partnered with all the TWS staff as we promoted legislation such as The Endangered American Wilderness Act and did scrappy organizing around RARE II (the Second Roadless Area Review and Evaluation) and the Bureau of Land Management wilderness review.

The network of Sierra Club and TWS organizers and lobbyists was dynamic, innovative, sometimes dangerous, highly effective, and lots of fun. It was a sad and painful period when William Turnage took over as Executive Director of TWS and decided to "professionalize" the staff so that all the scrappy, poorly paid grassroots-oriented organizers quit or were fired and replaced by polished white paper writers, lobbyists, and publicists. As Dave and the entire Western TWS organizing staff were hollowed out, TWS ceased to be an effective voice or presence outside of Washington, D.C. I quit my membership then and have never renewed.

My wife and I lived in an old, sagging, small log cabin outside Lander, Wyoming, at the time. I remember a day when Bart Koehler, Howie Wolke, and Mike Roselle came by for dinner and beers after returning from a long trip to Mexico. They told us about their trip to Mexico with Dave to rethink their futures and the future of the environmental movement. They railed about the sad fate of TWS, but they also expressed excitement about starting up some new group they would call Earth First! It would be the opposite of the new professional TWS—dirt bag, unapologetic, no compromise, no suits and ties, no big donors or foundation ties, and no compromise in defense of Mother Earth.

Dave and Dave Brower © David J. Cross, Dave Foreman Collection
California Wilderness Conference, 1985

Later that year, we all attended the first Earth First! Round River Rendezvous at the T-Cross Ranch outside of Dubois, WY. Around the campfire and over a few too many beers, Dave, Bart, and other TWS alumni pulled out their cloth embroidered Wilderness Society patches and symbolically wiped themselves and then burned them in the fire.

I had many long conversations with Dave over those Earth First! years as I continued to work for Sierra Club employing both the outside (organizing) and the inside (lobbying) games. Dave acknowledged that some good people had to be "in the room where it happens" to make sure the final deal was as strong as possible. He just did not want to be that person or to leave it up to TWS. He also had great admiration for wilderness warriors who actually spent weeks at a time out in the wilderness, and disdain for the full-time lobbyists and publicists who sat behind their desks while losing touch with the wild country that was being lost as deals were cut.

We all would joke about Monkey Wrenching and hang out with Ed Abbey, Doug Peacock, Ken Sleight, and other merry pranksters. Some of us went so far as to do some non-violent civil disobedience actions. Dave's middle-of-the-night arrest was a wakeup call that the federal government viewed Dave and Earth First! as a serious threat that had to be stamped out.

He became disenchanted with what Earth First! had evolved into and turned his attention to conservation biology, rewilding, and the idea of continental-scale core area and connectivity wildlands networks.

Around this same time, I was developing the Sierra Club's continental Critical Ecosystems Program that incorporated these ideas into our organizing vision. It was no longer sufficient to protect a small island of wilderness that could not support its native wildlife. We needed to link and protect from Yellowstone to Yukon and the Adirondacks to Acadia. Dave introduced me to great conservation biologists such as Michael Soulé and Reed Noss who were able to provide scientific backing for our wild-eyed dreams of land restoration and protection.

Conservation biology principles, inspired by Dave and his colleagues, were vital when I developed the Sierra Club's land protection program in response to the climate crisis—the Resilient Habitats Program. Again, the idea was protecting large core areas and connecting corridors to allow species to migrate and recover to adapt to climate change. They are now the foundation for the 30x30 and Nature Needs Half initiatives to address the biodiversity crisis in the midst of the climate crisis.

I became active in international wilderness protection through The WILD Foundation and the International Union for the Conservation of Nature. Through those efforts, I befriended Alec Marr, an Australian tree sitter and rabble-rouser who headed up the Australian Wilderness Society. Alec's organization was more like the Sierra Club than the US-based TWS—it took direct action, organized, got involved in electoral politics, and was not afraid to look and be radical. I introduced Alec to Dave and the Wildlands Network and soon a great partnership was set up. Michael Soulé went down to Australia and helped them set up a huge continental proposal for core areas and connecting corridors. It would not have happened without Dave's vision and connections.

Dave and his Wildlands Network and Rewilding colleagues also had a profound influence on my father, Dr. Lawrence Hamilton, who was the Vice President for Mountain Protected Areas of the International Union for the Conservation of Nature. Inspired by Dave's writings and the scientific papers of his conservation biology advisors, my father promoted a series of large core areas and connectivity corridors in the Andes, Alps, and Himalayas. Dave's "Path of the Panther" connectivity corridor in the Americas was duplicated around the globe.

When there was a vacancy on the Sierra Club Board of Directors due to a resignation, I asked Dave if he would be interested in serving, and he agreed to be appointed. His brief time on the Board was a challenging time, as the Board was wrestling with issues like a proposal (now policy) to support an end to all commercial logging on federal lands and draining Lake Powell and Hetch Hetchy reservoirs. Dave was very pragmatic, thoughtful, persuasive, and a great ally to me and the staff. He also worked with me to bring Michael Soulé to a Board retreat so they could all get a better understanding of the next phase of wildland protection that was necessary. While we disagreed strongly about the need for Sierra Club support for domestic immigration restrictions, we could agree that a Mexican wall was a terrible policy. The Sierra Club Board was not where Dave wanted to spend his time and energy, so he did not run for re-election when his term was up. He wanted to spend his time launching The Rewilding Institute and continuing to challenge all groups, including the Sierra Club, from the outside.

I remained in touch with Dave and would visit when I was in town. We would not only talk about wildlands politics and philosophy, but also about birds we had seen, and wild rivers we still needed to float. He had a misanthropic, gruff, and wild reputation and persona that people associate with him when he would spin yarns, spit out his outrage, and give off wolf howls. But once out of character, he was a kind, thoughtful, loving, and generous human being. I will always remember and honor him both ways.

Berkeley, CA
December 2022

Bruce Hamilton was the Field Editor of *High Country News* and held many positions in the Sierra Club for 45 years, from regional organizer to Conservation and Communications Director. He now volunteers for Third Act!, which organizes and empowers elders to take effective action on protecting democracy and reversing the climate crisis, and he spends as much free time as he can in wild places.

Foreman on the Front Lines

Art Goodtimes

He clung to the hood of the pickup
When the logger tried to run him down

Putting his wild life on the line
Standing in the path of the Machine

No small lawns of hope his vision
Nor bottom line profits uber alles

But an interwoven braid of all creation
Putting Earth's flora fauna & funga first

Protests, demos, monkeywrenching work
His was a Neo-Luddite path to change

Unfurling cracks in a dam, campfire songs
Blocking roads to the tallest redwoods

Hoping to turn our Titanic hubris away
From the looming icebergs of collapse

To show the titans of industry what radical
Really meant in defense of the Mother next

Inspiring a generation to rewild this blue planet
Using seeds of big ideas and small symbolic deeds

Aah, bless that good man. So many images. I can still see him gripping the hood of a logger's pickup that was trying to run him down. But a martini, enchiladas, and cherry pie. Damn. Dave knew how to live. And inspire us all. – Art

---

Noted poet, farmer, and San Miguel County, Colorado, County Commissioner for several years before retiring in 2016, Art Goodtimes is proud "that Dave saw the value of poetry and song and the arts in helping carry the message of Earth First!, *Wild Earth*, and The Rewilding Institute." He confirms that even Dave's woo-woo compatriots honor him for the courageous leader he has been. Art has received numerous prestigious awards for his activism and his poetry; he has been poet laureate of the Telluride Mushroom Festival for forty years.

L to R, Ron Kezar, Ken Sanders, Bart Koehler, Barb Steele, Howie Wolke, Nancy Morton, Dave Foreman, Mike Roselle, Shaaron Netherton, Roger Featherstone, kneeling, Gary Steele Earth First! group at Organ Pipe Cactus National Monument, 1985 © Dave Foreman Collection

Dave Foreman Has Gone Back to the Pleistocene

Jamie Sayen

The *New York Times* reported on September 28, 2022: "David Foreman, Hard-line Environmentalist, Dies at 75." The one-dimensional sensationalism of this obituary was inevitable, but it cheated readers of the *Times* out of an appreciation of the richness of Dave's life and his epoch-changing role in the New Conservation Movement.

The obituary opened: "David Foreman, who as the co-founder of the environmental group Earth First! urged his followers to sabotage bulldozers, slash logging-truck tires, and topple high-voltage power lines, earning him a reputation as a visionary, a rabble-rouser, a prankster and, even among some fellow activists, a domestic terrorist…"

The *Times'* failure to offer insight into a complex, controversial visionary who transformed the conservation of wild nature was a disservice to its readers.

Dave and others espoused monkeywrenching, or ecotage, because they were desperate. Industrial mining, forestry, agriculture, and wealthy vacationers were pulverizing wild nature. Mainstream conservation groups had grown cozy with exploitative corporations and government agencies charged with protecting the natural legacy of the United States.

When Dave and other Earth First! scruffians engaged in psychological warfare against the death machines, they used all tools available to defend one's family from a crazed intruder. Yes, they caused some economic damage, and yes, there were risks that ecotage could cause injury or fatality, but mostly they drove up the blood pressure of land plunderers. If corporate profits are more sanctified than wild, evolving life, then yes, they were outlaws.

But, what of the death of critters whose habitat had been clearcut, bulldozed, or poisoned? What of the fate of extirpated predators: cougar, wolf, lynx, even wolverine? What of the health of our life-supporting planet? In warfare, it is always the innocent who suffer the most. Dave stood up for the innocents—non-human and human alike.

Earth First! and monkeywrenching were Dave's first act in transforming how we perform conservation in America, and throughout the world. Sadly, the *Times* missed the fascinating growth and development of Dave into one of the great conservation thinkers and leaders ever.

Dave and the early Earth-First!ers were desperate to transform conservation from a political exercise into an ecologically-informed practice. With the conservation-industrial complex deaf to their pleas, wilderness defenders resorted to radical proclamations and actions that seized everyone's attention. As the message about uncompromising defense of Mother Earth spread, growing numbers of conservationists and conservation scientists joined the chorus.

Once you have the attention of the public, you do not need to shout from rooftops. It is time to move beyond bumper stickers (although Earth First!

offered the best: Equal Rights for All Species; Nature Bats Last; American Wilderness: Love it or Leave it Alone; Neanderthal and Proud).

With a national bully pulpit, Dave's career blossomed. In 1983, he mapped existing roadless areas and published a potential Wilderness Map of the United States in *Earth First! Journal.* In the mid-1980s, *Earth First!* began to evolve into a cutting-edge journal espousing activism informed by conservation science.

I met Dave at the 1985 Round River Rendezvous in the Uncompahgre National Forest in Colorado. Dave was a generous guy, and when I admired his traveling library of field guides, he loaned me one. One evening, after dinner, we gathered around the communal campfire, and Dave challenged us to act out our totem species. Many of us offered goofball parodies of our totem. A few, more attentive folks realistically portrayed their species' behavioral traits. It was a hilarious and instructive experience.

The following winter, Dave convened a Grizz Task Force meeting at Larry Campbell and Marty Almquist's beautiful log cabin in Darby, Montana. A dozen Earth First! activists and experts came together to develop a Grizzly Bear Recovery Plan. I was living in Larry and Marty's old stackwood house, and I volunteered to be chief dishwasher so I could eavesdrop on the proceedings.

That weekend I learned that Earth-First!ers were well-informed, creative-thinking activists. Dave, in particular, stood out as the person with the clearest understanding of the challenges the bears faced and the direction activists should take. In day-long sessions, he facilitated thoughtful discussions that led us to promising strategies for their recovery.

In the evenings, this eclectic group broke out the beer and regaled one another with tall stories. One evening, as Dave was telling me about his recent conversion to fine wines, Howie and Doug engaged in a wrestling match to the death in the small living room. Earth First!—for the erudite and the primal.

At some point, I wrote Dave an enthusiastic letter, asking: Why doesn't Earth First! do more in the Eastern states? He responded as always, "If you want Earth First! to be active in your area, get moving."

In the fall of 1986, I bought a log cabin in the backwoods of northern New Hampshire. To celebrate, I went backpacking in the White Mountains.

On a raw, socked-in day, fighting hypothermia on the Franconia Ridge Trail, a section of the Appalachian Trail, I pondered the paucity of wilderness in the Eastern United States. It occurred to me that the Appalachian Trail, connecting Springer Mountain in northern Georgia with Mt. Katahdin in northern Maine, could provide a wilderness backbone to link core wilderness areas throughout the Appalachian Mountains with Florida and eastern Canada.

I wrote a letter to the *EF! Journal*, briefly outlining my idea. Dave challenged me to submit an article. I spent a very cold winter in my new, leaky cabin, huddled by an inefficient cook stove, burning green firewood I'd cut the day before, writing a long, undisciplined proposal to Preserve Appalachian Wilderness (PAW). Dave and John Davis published it in the May 1987 issue. I formed a group to promote the idea and called it PAW.

The following winter, Dave invited me to join him at a New Age retreat in western Massachusetts, the Rowe Conference Center, to put on an EF! activists weekend workshop. I had no idea what this meant but was happy to tag along.

Dave enthralled the 30 or so attendees, including several New England EF! activists. As the weekend wound down, Dave challenged us to come up with an "Action." After some mumbling and bumbling, someone suggested we dramatize the plight of the Connecticut River strain of the Atlantic salmon. A voice piped up, "We could dress as salmon and paddle upstream to dramatize all the obstacles the once abundant salmon encounter on their journey from sea to spawning bed." Before the weekend ended, we had formed the Salmon Revival Run (SRR).

A modest group of salmon launched the SRR on Memorial Day 1988. For the next five weeks, we paddled up the Connecticut whose strong currents had largely been tamed by a series of dams. We passed by large marinas in southern Connecticut, two nuclear power plants, agricultural fields leaching toxins into the river, and several stretches with scant evidence of human development.

Prior to the passage of the Clean Water Act of 1972, municipalities, factories, and farms had dumped their waste into the 400-mile Connecticut, earning it the title of "The Most Beautiful Sewer in the World." Canoe paddles brought up toilet paper, and foul fumes sickened the paddlers. By 1988, the

Connecticut was clean enough for swimming, a blessing in that torrid, global warming summer.

The daily rhythmic paddling and the surviving wild beauty of the river seduced us. By the time we disbanded after traveling over 200 miles, I had discovered that despite dams, development, and degradation, the wildness remained. Even the most abused ecosystem can heal itself if we mortals will only refrain from obstructing natural processes. I suspect the Salmon Revival Run was but one of scores of adventures and challenges that Dave inspired over the years. *Dave the catalyst!*

In the spring of 1989, Dave took a hit for the Earth First! movement. The FBI set Dave up for allegedly plotting with some northern Arizona activists to topple a powerline. At the Round River Rendezvous that June, Dave, facing the threat of years in jail, was exhausted, but, as ever, focused on wildlands and rewilding.

As the 1980s wore on, Earth First! grew in prominence and notoriety, and tribal squabbling metastasized into schism. Dave's controversial comments about overpopulation and other issues infuriated many leftist EF!ers. Dave pled with us to debate our philosophic differences respectfully, but the rancor intensified.

By 1990, the schism in Earth First! had worn him down, and he and Nancy resigned from the movement he had co-founded. Over the next year, Dave focused on launching what he referred to as the "New Conservation Movement." In the spring of 1991, Dave and John Davis, an unsung hero of the New Conservation Movement, launched *Wild Earth*, a quarterly journal dedicated to staving off the Sixth Extinction Event. *Wild Earth* brought about, in Dave's words, a "marriage of activism and conservation biology." It represented a maturing of the Earth First! movement: no compromise activism informed and guided by cutting-edge conservation science.

In November 1991, Dave and wildlands philanthropist, Doug Tompkins, invited a dozen North American wildlands activists and conservation biologists to San Francisco for a weekend brainstorming session that gave birth to The Wildlands Project (later renamed The Wildlands Network), an organization dedicated to developing a North American Wilderness Recovery Strategy. He would later describe TWP as a continental scale network that sets the New Conservation agenda: the development of a disciplined strategy to rewild whole ecosystems and landscapes and bring back extirpated large predators.

Dave's genius in marrying uncompromising activism with conservation science has broader ramifications. Conservation science lays out the natural laws and limits that define the parameters of our economic, social, political, and cultural aspirations. Respect natural limits, as Mr. Micawber might observe: "result happiness;" transgress those limits: "result misery," and relentless transgressions: result climate and extinction crises.

A deeper lesson is: all is not political. Our politics must defer to natural and physical limits we are powerless to repeal or evade. Thus, our economic debates are not primarily of a political nature. The political debates over economic options are only valid within natural limits. Step one is always: what activities and aspirations complement natural and physical limits?

Political and economic powers possess the short-term power to ignore, evade, and violate limits, but they are powerless to get away with such ignorance. Most political decisions come down to opinions, ideology, aspirations, and who has the power to get their way. I find it liberating that neither I nor any living being has the power to overrule or evade natural laws. By marrying uncompromising activism with conservation and climate science, Dave taught us that conservationists wield power that has been denied to all would-be world conquerors, from Alexander and Caesar down to Napoleon.

To the end, Dave was the truest of conservatives: a creative, courageous man who gave his life to the conservation of billions of years of evolving, wild life.

Dave's final journey has taken him back to the Pleistocene. Happy trails, Dave.

Jamie Sayen is the author of *You Had a Job for Life*, an oral history of the defunct Groveton, NH, paper mill, published in 2018 and to be re-released by Brandeis University Press in the Fall of 2023. His new book, *Children of the Northern Forest*, the story of the Acadian Forest of northern New England, will be published by Yale University Press in the Fall of 2023. He lives in northern New Hampshire.

Dave Foreman: A Great Bio-Ethicist Who Stood Strong

Jack Loeffler

Dave Foreman and I first crossed trails in 1971. He was then a burgeoning environmentalist with tremendous imagination, and I was manning the Black Mesa Defense Fund (BMFD), an early eco-anarchist alliance working at the behest of Hopi traditional Indians to try to halt the strip-mining of coal from Black Mesa, a landform sacred to Hopi and Navajo cultures. We were also attempting to thwart the construction of more coal-fired power plants on the Colorado Plateau. Dave did volunteer work for both the BMDF and the Central Clearing House, another Santa Fe environmental group. He thereafter put in eight years working for The Wilderness Society. In 1984, I recorded Dave Foreman addressing his work as an environmentalist.

> **Dave Foreman:** "I basically came to the conclusion that we were being co-opted by the establishment, that having influence and all made us more moderate. We compromised more, thought about pragmatic politics instead of biocentric ethics.... We decided that the time had come for an environmental group that wouldn't compromise, that would base itself on ethics instead of pragmatics, and that would take strong action to try to stop the destruction of wilderness.... We've had people go in and stand in front of bulldozers constructing logging roads into wild areas. We've had people sit in dynamite-loaded fields to stop mountains from being blown away. We've hugged trees to keep trees from being cut down by chainsaws.... We are Earth First!"

Thus, Dave Foreman and a group of fellow stalwarts set a mighty new standard among environmentalists. They spiked trees to protect them from sawmill blades. But they identified the trees they spiked to avoid harm to fellow humans. They pulled up survey stakes and closed roads that didn't belong. They used imagination and enormous courage in defense of Mother Earth.

> **Dave Foreman:** "If you look at the human race not as the consciousness of the Earth, but as a cancer of the Earth—that we're a disease ecologically—that maybe Nature has evolved some of us as antibodies.... There are really two things I'm trying to do in the long term. One is to lay the groundwork for a human society in the future that is ecologically based, and the other is to preserve as much natural diversity now as we can....
>
> Everything has intrinsic value. You don't preserve wilderness because you like to hike in it or because it is pretty to look at. You preserve wilderness for its own sake....And if you want to take it even further, a species of mosquito is just as important as the human species is—that what's really important is not the individual or the species, but the community, the interlocking of different life forms and what we call inanimate objects that make up a community in a stable, diverse, healthy ecosystem. That's really where evolution takes place, that's really where the life force is."

One of Dave's great friends and mentors was author/anarchist Edward Abbey. Ed held Dave Foreman in highest regard. Earth First! house was located within a few miles of Abbey's home on the western edge of Tucson. Indeed, Ed made many presentations at Earth First! house including his last public reading from the final manuscript of *Hayduke Lives!* a week before he died on March 14, 1989.

On January 1, 1983, Ed and I were returning from a week-or-so-long camping trip in the Superstition Mountains. For six months, we knew of the malaise that would eventually carry him away. We decided that I should record him when we got back to his writing cabin west of his home in Tucson where

Jack Loeffler, Dave Petersen, Bart Koehler, and Dave, in Durango Celebrating Ed Abbey, circa 2002 © Dave Foreman Collection

I'd stashed my recording equipment. We talked of many things including the terms 'sabotage' and 'ecoterrorism.'

> **Ed Abbey:** "The distinction is quite clear and simple. Sabotage is an act of force or violence against material objects, machinery, in which life is not endangered or should not be. Terrorism, on the other hand, is violence against living things—human beings and other living things. That kind of terrorism is generally practiced by governments against their own peoples.... Our government committed great acts of terrorism against the people of Vietnam.... I'd go so far as to say that a bulldozer tearing up hillside, ripping out trees for a logging operation or strip mine is committing terrorism—violence against life."

Ed Abbey was a strong advocate for civil disobedience in his determination to protect landscapes that he loved.

> **Ed Abbey:** "If civil disobedience is not enough, I imagine there will be sabotage, violence against machinery, property. Those are desperate measures. If they become widespread, it could be that the battle has already been lost.... Such resistance might stimulate some sort of police-state reaction, repression, a real military-industrial dictatorship in this country."

In the meantime, Earth First! and Dave Foreman were making the establishment ever more uneasy. Six weeks after Abbey's death in 1989, FBI agents barged into the Foreman bedroom where Dave and his wife Nancy were still asleep in the pre-dawn.

The agents aimed their pistols at Dave, gruffly rousted him out of bed, and arrested him on charges that were invented as part of the entrapment they had initiated many months earlier with the infiltration of an agent into Earth First!. The spy's name was Michael Fain, (he used the name Mike Tait), and he spent months secretly taping conversations with Dave, ever trying to get Dave to admit to committing or inciting sabotage. I know this to be true because I was asked by Sam Guiberson, one of Dave's defense attorneys, who had obtained a court order to make a duplicate set of over 60 hours of tape recordings of these conversations, as well as recordings of bugged telephone conversations. I listened to every word and know for a fact that Dave never admitted to anything that was against the law. From my point of view, this was an attempt at entrapment.

Shortly after his arrest, Dave called me and asked me over the phone if I would head up his defense fund. I agreed immediately, although I'm no great shakes as a fund raiser. But with a lot of help from folks all over the country, some famous, others ardent in their environmentalism, we were able to raise the funding necessary to proceed with Dave's defense.

I had searched for an organization with a 501c(3) to accept non-taxable donations. The only positive response I received was from Dave Brower, who had recently founded Earth Island Institute. When the trial was to begin in Prescott, Arizona, Brower called me and said we had to be there together to provide moral support. We arrived in Prescott but were not allowed in the courtroom. Thus, we waited out that day of the trial in a tavern across the street from the courthouse, where we were joined by Doug Peacock, another hardcore environmentalist.

After plea bargaining, Dave pled guilty to one count of conspiracy, though he received no prison sentence. (There's another story there that is not mine to tell.) He was vigorously urged by the establishment to change his style of defense of Mother Earth. After five years, his charge was changed to a misdemeanor, he was fined $250, and he thus became free to pursue his own brilliant style of activism on behalf of wilderness preservation.

It was then that I personally realized that human legislation is often in violation of natural law. This begs the question: "Whose law do you abide by, or do I abide by? Human legislation that favors turning habitat into money? Or natural law which now actively decrees otherwise?" Think global warming.

Meanwhile, Foreman continued to pursue preservation of wilderness full tilt.

Dave Foreman: "I think wilderness is one of those words that needs to be clearly defined because a lot of the wrangle over conservation is based upon poor understandings of what wilderness really means. If we go really far back in the English language before it was even English, we find that the word wilderness comes from three words: will – der – ness, which translates literally as "the will of the land" or self-willed land. I think that that is the most important meaning of wilderness, that it's land with its own will, as contrasted to civilized landscapes that are primarily under human will. To recognize the value of self-willed land is a really major step of humility. I think the whole conservation battle for 150 years in the United States and elsewhere around the world has been over this idea of self-willed land. Those who would just go in and exploit land, whether to log it off, graze it off, trap it out, dry up the rivers with no thought of sustainability—that looting kind of mentality—is one of imposing human will on the land but without caring for the future.

If we look at what's happened to North America since Europeans have been here, the stripping off of forests, the trapping out of wildlife, shooting off of game—passenger pigeon, bison—the overgrazing, all of that has been done with a looting mentality of imposing human will on a landscape by just getting what's good while the gettin's good and moving on with no thought of sustainability. That's a classic sort of philosophy of imposing human will on the land. When Gifford Pinchot and the Forest Service came in, they still wanted to impose human will on the land, but they wanted to do it in an efficient, sustainable manner. But conservation, I think, has fundamentally been about respecting self-willed land and saying that we needed to protect some land with a will of its own for its own sake, where conservation is fundamentally about respecting self-willed land and recognizing that we need to step back and have humility to let some land have its own will to be itself.

This is another important role of large carnivores like grizzly bears or wolves or mountain lions. Those who would destroy them and dislike their presence and don't want to let wolves back, it's primarily over what kind of will is going to be in the lion. A mountain lion or a wolf is a *wildeor*, a self-willed animal, in old English. If you want to impose human will on the land, you want to get rid of those kinds of critters that have their own will. So I think the fundamental struggle in conservation and about protecting wilderness areas and about protecting wolves and bears and mountain lions is about respecting self-willed land and having the humility to say that we need to leave some land free of our will and domination....

Michael Soulé calls wilderness areas self-regulated ecosystems, which means the same thing as self-willed land. The Wilderness Act uses a somewhat obscure term, 'untrammeled,' to refer to wilderness areas. Well, a trammel in Old French was a hobble on a horse or a fishing net. So to trammel something meant to control it, to impose your own will on it. So untrammeled land as used in the Wilderness Act is self-willed land. So all of these meanings, whether recreational or experiential, I think come together in the original meaning of wilderness, will of the land. That's what the fight is all about. Do we have the generosity of spirit and the greatness of heart to recognize that there are places that we should not impose our will on, that there are critters out there whose only fault is that they don't get along with us and do well in our human-willed landscapes? What it comes down to is humility."

The above is excerpted from a conversation I recorded with Dave on November 12, 1999.

In 2008, I was producing an hour-long radio documentary about Aldo Leopold in the Southwest. I knew that Dave Foreman had been greatly influenced by Leopold and thus recorded yet another interview with him, an excerpt from which I include here.

Dave Foreman: "Going to work for the Wilderness Society in 1973 as the Southwest representative was such a connection for me. And my view of conservation is that conservation is a family of Nature-lovers, where today it seems to be a collection of institutions which really bothers me. To me, the Wilderness Society in those days was still a family and being made a part of that family was such an enormous honor and treat for me, particularly working within the Southwest where Aldo Leopold had worked on the Gila Wilderness, and finally seeing the wilderness enlarged in 1980 thanks to Pete Domenici and Manny Lujan who I worked really closely with on the legislation, and having us get stuff included in the wilderness that the Forest Service had been trying to keep out of the wilderness since 1952. That was in many ways the great achievement I had in the 1970s working on the wilderness. Also being shaped by Leopold's evolving attitudes toward wilderness because when he first proposed wilderness areas—I think it was in the early '20s he wrote an article, a plea to preserve roadless camping grounds for horseback travel and all. It was entirely a recreational thing. He saw wilderness areas as a place to provide an opportunity for primitive travel and living, and even saw the ranches that were still there, and what he proposed for the Gila Wilderness was some kind of frontier experience for visitors.

But by the late '30s, and his involvement with pioneering ecologists, he had come around to a very ecological view of wilderness where he wrote that 'wilderness is the theater of evolution' which I think is really the fundamental idea behind protecting wilderness areas where you're protecting a place for evolution. And Leopold was about the first person to talk about that, and so seeing evolution from wilderness strictly being a place for primitive travel in reaction to automobiles to being the theater for evolution and a reserve for evolution with all its different parts to continue on is I think the essence of the wilderness area idea."

Dave Foreman was a fine scholar of ecology and environmental thinking and had that rare capacity for refining and integrating his vast knowledge into direct action. As many of us know, he didn't restrict himself to the comfortable indoors. He was a great outdoorsman, a back-packer, and river-runner. He and his wife Nancy Morton were a team, both as environmental activists and in backcountry wilderness.

I was fortunate to have run both Desolation Canyon and the San Juan River with Dave and Nancy and found them to be delightful to camp with and to know as fellow humans. My half-century friendship with Dave Foreman is an honored memory.

Adios, muchacho…

Postscript: The FBI spy behind Dave's arrest was recording, and inadvertently recorded himself, as was revealed in the trial. "I don't really look for them to be doing a lot of hurting people... [Foreman] isn't really the guy we need to pop—I mean in terms of an actual perpetrator. This is the guy we need to pop to send a message. And that's all we're really doing... Uh-oh! We don't need that on tape! Hoo boy!" But it was on tape, confirming the FBI entrapment scheme. One of the group arrested in the incident, who was engaging in ecotage, was Peg Millet, who was sentenced to three years and restitution of $19,821…. Dave Foreman's case was separated from the other four and sentencing was deferred until 1996, when the charges were reduced to a single misdemeanor and he was fined $250. Attorney, colleague, and friend of Dave's, David Johns, wrote to me: "Dear Jack: They would not allow Dave to sever his case until he had agreed to a plea deal. It was all or nothing. That was their lever. Because the others were facing major time, he was under enormous pressure and did agree to a plea. Part of the deal was that not until after five years of 'good behavior' was the charge against him reduced to a misdemeanor. Best, David Johns."

Jack Loeffler is a lifelong outdoorsman, hiking and camping extensively throughout the American West and Mexico and rafting many rivers. During the 1960s, he was a fire lookout in the Carson National Forest. In 1970, he co-founded the Central Clearing House that documented environmentally endangered hotspots in the Southwest, and the Black Mesa Defense Fund, an early radical environmental group that worked closely with traditional Hopi Indians to attempt to thwart the strip-mining of coal at Black Mesa, a landform sacred to both Hopi and Navajo Indians. He has been awarded many grants to proceed as a self-styled aural historian, visiting and often living in native villages and visiting academic and scientific communities to conduct interviews. He has extensively recorded the music and lore of indigenous peoples and their biotic communities and has trained indigenous peoples to record traditional elders to preserve oral tradition. Using his own recordings, he has produced more than 300 documentary radio programs for Public Radio and many sound collages for museums. He has written many books and scores of essays. He has donated his aural history archive to the New Mexico History Museum in Santa Fe. He has lived in rural northern New Mexico for sixty years.

A Leap of Faith: The Wildlands Project

On November 20 and 21, 1991, fifteen grassroots wilderness activists, academicians, and conservation biologists met at Doug Tompkins' house in San Francisco. Dave called the meeting, and Rod Mondt organized it. During the previous couple of years, Dave had been talking to friends and associates about a new kind of wilderness organization, and he finally had enough ideas and people to begin planning. Out of discussions at this gathering grew an outfit that was incorporated under the name of North American Wilderness Recovery, Inc. A board of directors was established, and the new organization was eventually renamed The Wildlands Project (TWP). Dave credited Doug Tompkins, founder and director of the Foundation for Deep Ecology, for initiating the November meeting. It was Doug's boundless energy, enthusiasm, prodding, and funding that encouraged him and others that the time had come to stop talking and act. Dave and Doug were big thinkers and impatient actors and knew there was no time to lose to get big things done. Doug, of course, went on to do incredible conservation work in South America, protecting and rewilding vast landscapes with the help of his wife Kris, principally in Argentina and Chile.

The Wildlands Project evolved out of the traditional wilderness movement and the discipline of conservation biology. Out of these roots came the Project's blended strategy of advocacy and science and its vision to protect vast, interconnected areas of true wilderness and the network of life that wilderness supports.

Wild Earth Journal, which would become the publication that nurtured and reported the work of the "new conservation movement" exemplified by The Wildlands Project, published its first issue even before the San Francisco meeting. Allied with but independent of TWP, it was where "Big Thinkers, Wild Thoughts" could be shared free of any editorial or managerial constraints from TWP. *Wild Earth's* publisher was Dave Foreman, and its very capable editors over the years were John Davis and Tom Butler. This publication, a hybrid including academic papers, reporting, wonderful illustrations, and themed issues, set new journalistic standards in conservation and environmental education until WE announced "the end of an era" with the fall/winter 2004-2005 issue when it ceased publication. Even though the funding between the journal and TWP had been kept separate, the difficult decision was made that ending publication would allow more resources to be directed to conservation programs, which would leave a "void in the global conversation on conservation." It certainly did.

Meanwhile, in order to reach The Wildlands Project's "big and bold" ecological goals of restoring and reconnecting large tracts of wildlands in North America, TWP founders devised a land conservation strategy based on biodiversity and wildness. Reed Noss was the chief architect, and it was born principally out of conservation biology. TWP's vision, goals, and mission statement married science with ideas and advocacy from the traditional wilderness movement, which had been carried forward from Earth First!.

At this stage of his career, Dave was content to work more behind the scenes than he had with Earth First!. His fertile mind and booming voice were influential in TWP deliberations, and he continued to organize and speak and write. To some extent, he was the voice of The Wildlands Project. His extensive travels with the EF! Road Show, and a demanding speaking schedule for years, had given him knowledge not only of North American wildland geography but also of the many grassroots groups working across the land to address goals important to TWP plans. He helped build collaborations with these groups, and he occasionally reminded his TWP colleagues not to overlook the value, insights, and contributions that grassroots and indigenous groups who knew their homelands could bring to the planning process.

In the ensuing years, the board and staff worked with the processes of reserve design, components of a reserve network—core areas, buffer zones, and connectivity—and vision mapping that was eventually drafted into a continental reserve design. Dave, with his love of maps, encyclopedic knowledge of wildlands remaining in North America derived from his extensive research with Howie Wolke for their book *The Big Outside*, and his growing understanding of the concepts and insights of conservation biology, worked with Reed, Michael Soulé, and others on wildland network designs and gradually a continental network VISION emerged. This work was not accomplished without challenges. TWP was seen by some in the "environmental" community as "too grandiose" and by others as not focused enough on animal rights, social justice, or cultural health issues. And even though TWP was built on a history of traditional wilderness advocacy, some in the traditional wilderness community were offended that TWP changed the course of conservation. TWP moved the emphasis in wildland protection from the traditional rationales focused on protecting scenery and wildland recreation to scientifically based rationales aimed at protecting biological diversity. Their approach also served as a counter to postmodern conservationists, who denied the very existence of wild nature.

Michael Soulé affirmed all along that TWP must hold firmly to its "unflinching vision." Andy Robinson, development staff for TWP, stated that the organization "continued to bring together conservation activists and scientists to create and implement a long-term vision of a biologically healthy continent, with enough wilderness to support the full diversity of plant and animal life." Within conservation and scientific communities, biodiversity and support for big, bold designs were finally given primary consideration in conservation planning.

Michael Soulé believed The Wildlands Project was the most creative organization he had been associated with—experimenting, testing, and monitoring its progress very much like it must check the theories of conservation biology. TWP served as a catalyst through *Wild Earth* and by working with cooperating organizations. As TWP grew, long-time friends and collaborators in the board and staff reassessed and reorganized from time to time. In 1996, the "charismatic megafounder" became Chairman of the Board where he stayed until 2003 to establish The Rewilding Institute.

One of Dave's insights that had percolated in his thinking since the mid-1980s was that not only should all the remaining wildland in North America be protected, but much of the landscape that had been degraded in one way or another should be "rewilded." He coined this term, which caught on and is used variously in conservation conversations around the world. There was more work to do than simply connecting existing wildlands—more wildlands could and should be restored in North America and elsewhere across the world. He did not believe that when wildland was degraded or tamed, it was gone forever. Also, not all land valuable to protection needs to be wilderness though he was the strongest, or at least the most vocal, advocate for "wildeor," self-willed land and wildlife, wherever they could be preserved. He had a lot to share with his colleagues in TWP.

In a special issue of *Wild Earth* in 1992, focused on The Wildlands Project, Reed Noss reviewed the available evidence on how much protected land is required to meet ambitious but necessary conservation goals. He concluded that "each region must be assessed individually," but that as a generalization, "at least half of the land area of the 48 conterminous states should be encompassed in core reserves and inner corridor zones…within the next few decades." Noss was the first to make the argument for 50% protection (or 25-75%, depending on the region) based on biodiversity goals, but in his article, he quoted the pioneering work of eminent ecologist brothers Eugene and Howard T. Odum. Fully two decades before Noss's article, the Odums completed a systems ecology study of South Florida to determine how much natural area must be retained to provide what we now call "ecosystem services" to human society. They concluded from their model that "a 1:1 ratio of natural to developed environment would provide a basis for an optimum environmental-use program" for South Florida. They followed with a general recommendation: "Until this kind of systems analysis procedure can be refined and becomes a basis for political action, it would be prudent for planners everywhere to strive to preserve 50 percent of the total environment as natural environment." Following the visionary work of the Odums in 1972 and Noss in 1992, Canadian conservationist Harvey Locke widely promoted the idea of "Nature needs half" to an international audience, beginning with an article in *The George Wright Forum* in 2014. Two years later, Ed Wilson published *Half Earth* and is usually given the credit for originating this idea.

Time has confirmed the significance of The Wildlands Project and the work it has done and is doing. Conservation biology has continued to advance as an applied science. The problems of climate change and threats to biological diversity have risen to the top of the global conservation agenda. Today, the ideas of protecting 30% of the Earth by 2030 and 50% by 2050 have caught on globally, and much work is underway to accomplish these goals, which would have been inconceivable when Dave Foreman began his conservation career in the late 1970s. Whether the goals are achievable remains to be seen, but Dave and his TWP colleagues played an important role in thinking and planning on such scales.

Goodbye, Dave, We Love and Thank You...

Kris Tompkins

It's impossible to separate the work Doug and I and our teams have done in conservation over the last 30 years in the absence of Dave Foreman. Of course, there were others before Dave who understood the intrinsic value of all life; who understood, even at the turn of the 20th century, that if we did not save the important ecosystems on earth, we would find ourselves living and dying in a barren landscape. But for our generation, Dave was and will continue to be, that insistent, strident voice who put civil action together with the sentiment to keep your hands off key territories and preserve the wildlands that still remain. There will be much written about Earth First! and the building of a movement that drew the line in the sand over what land and sea territories shall be converted to production and what has to be saved from what Doug always called *"The Price of Progress."* It is clear today that though the effects of changes in climate are causing untold levels of human and non-human suffering, the will to do anything about it is dwindling at its core—the absence of the clear, direct voices that Dave represented at the height of his activism are missing at this most critical time.

In 1990, Dave, Michael Soulé, Reed Noss, John Terborgh, and others joined with Doug Tompkins to form an entity specifically charged with identifying the key habitat in North America and focused on the new thinking of how to connect these territories together such that wildlife could migrate from one region to another. It was imperative to have a vision for what lands really were essential if we have any hope of protecting wildlife and wildlands in North America. Groundwork that all conservationists around the world depend on today was crafted by this extraordinary group, The Wildlands Project. Dave Foreman was central to this vision, and it is the debt we owe to him and to all members of this tribe.

L to R standing: Roz McClellan, John Davis, David Johns, Jim Eaton, Doug Tompkins, Dave Foreman, George Wuerthner, Mitch Friedman, Monte Hummel, Jamie Sayen, Rod Mondt, Reed Noss, kneeling: Michael Soulé
TWP Founders, 1991 © George Wuerthner

I have felt the loss of so many friends and fellow fighters for the Wild this year—Bill Conway, EO Wilson, Tom Lovejoy, Howard Quigley, and now Dave. Though there are many younger biologists, naturalists, and conservationists working around the world today, the rapid loss of so many of those original thinkers, the people who were in the field for decades; learning to see, firsthand what it was they were looking at. These people have informed what will be generations of those who are coming up now and into the future—our deep understanding of ecosystems, bio-regions, the fabric of how all life winds itself together, and, most difficult of all, how to express our human impacts on an ecological system that is at once capable of evolving infinitely and yet, fragile enough to be the brunt of the loss of our human capacity to see ourselves as part of a whole, not at the center but rather on the edges, and our life depends on this. Dave Foreman used every last ounce he had to champion the rights of wildness and the values of beauty and the costs of our unwillingness to fight every day to change the end of this story. He will remain much missed for a very long, long time.

Kristine McDivitt Tompkins, former CEO of the Patagonia clothing company, is the co-founder and president of Tompkins Conservation. She was a key figure behind the establishment of Monte León National Park in Argentina and Patagonia National Park in Chile, as well as other conservation projects. For decades she also worked with her husband, Doug Tompkins, to model a new agroecological paradigm by operating organic farms and ranches in Chile and Argentina. She serves in various positions of global leadership in conservation, including as Chair of National Geographic Society's Last Wild Places campaign. She received the Carnegie Medal of Philanthropy in 2017 and was named the UN Environment Patron of Protected Areas in 2018.

Dave Foreman's Legacy

David Johns

One of the most passionate, creative, and dedicated advocates for the wild slipped away from us recently (September 19, 2022). It's not just a personal loss, though that is deeply felt. I worked closely with Dave Foreman to fight the U.S. attempt to intimidate and silence him in the late 80s and early 90s. We floated many rivers and hiked many trails. Dave and Nancy attended my wedding at Big Camp on the Imnaha River in Eagle Cap Wilderness. It was sunny, rained, hailed, and even snowed briefly that August. Wild weather. Dave swing-danced his way through much of the event.

That was thirty years ago when we started The Wildlands Network with Reed Noss, George Wuerthner, Doug Tompkins, and several others. It was a heady time. Globally and in the US, conservation was inadequate to the challenge of growing extinction, habitat loss and fragmentation, and disruption of natural processes. Never satisfied with defense—which he considered a losing approach—he recognized the imperative of the offense—creating and implementing a positive vision of large, connected reserves adequate to support healthy populations of all native species, including top carnivores, to allow the processes of evolution to operate unencumbered and be resilient to periodic human disturbances.

In short, he proposed that we do what was needed, not what was possible. Changing what is possible went much slower than we hoped. The opposition was strong and well-entrenched, and potential allies extremely cautious. If Half Earth is part of the discussion today, it was revolutionary when first advanced in the 1990s. (EO Wilson endorsed our work in 1994.) With some exceptions (such as Patagonia, Gorongosa, and others) we are not as far along as we should be. Extinction is now; climate change is now. 8 billion is now. Cars, cell phones, and tons of plastics are now. Mass human recalcitrance, denial, and obliviousness are now.

Dave never deluded himself about the state of things. The brutally ugly reality of industrial civilization grinding up life's beauty weighed heavily on him. There were no quick fixes, only organized political action could change things—a difficult task he continually set himself and colleagues to.

Speaking at a large professional meeting, writer and activist Terry Tempest Williams ruffled some staid scientific feathers when she said that we needed to be as fierce defending nature as a mother griz defending her cubs. It wasn't enough to document decline and putter around the edges. Dave shared her view and was fierce in his work. Like Bob Marshall, long ago Wilderness Society co-founder, he did not tolerate fence straddlers or those who wanted peace above all else. That was the point of Earth First! in its first decade—to actually put the Earth and its millions of species first in our embrace, values, and action. He recognized that humans were only one species among many and not the center of the universe—though they behaved as if they were. The horror of the mass infliction of suffering on creation due to human myopia, greed, and inertia caused him to frequently mention in his talks Leopold's statement about living in a world of wounds.

Dave drew strength from his time in the wild. He also drew strength from the rich web of conservationists that grew around him. The web is frayed a bit with his death. It can't be patched, but as with all losses, colleagues—in part because of his inspiration that lives on—must learn to work around his immense loss. As Dave is mourned and tears shed, the resolve to continue the fight ever more effectively grows. Dave gave voice to and embodied a movement; he helped to lead it. That voice lives on in his speeches, books, campfire columns, and time spent with countless conservationists around real campfires.

It lives on in The Rewilding Institute: keeping the flame burning through its commitment to restoring whole systems of self-willed lands, waters, and creatures, and settling for nothing less; addressing the causes of decline—endless human population growth, endless economic growth, and advocating what is necessary for wildlife and places to thrive. Too many NGOs handicap themselves by embracing the status quo to gain acceptance, rather than transcending it. It cannot be business as usual. For several decades many have talked about having a decade left to make a major course correction in the human trajectory. That decade has come and gone several times. Circumstances are urgent.

Dave's death reminds us of that and urges us on.

David Johns has advocated for large-scale conservation for many decades. A co-founder of The Wildlands Network, Yellowstone to Yukon Conservation Initiative, and Conservation Biology Institute, he currently serves as secretary of the Marine Conservation Institute, which is home to the Blue Parks Initiative, and he is on the board of The Rewilding Institute. He has worked on conservation projects throughout the Americas, in the Russian Far East, Australia, Europe, southern Africa, and the global ocean. An activist, attorney, and conservation strategist, he is the author of *A New Conservation Politics* (2009), a manual on effective conservation advocacy, and *Conservation Politics: The Last Anti-Colonial Battle* (2019), about overcoming the root causes of ecological decline instead of treating symptoms. He taught politics and law at Portland State University as an adjunct for 40 years.

L to R, Unidentified, Dale Turner, Michael Soulé, Reed Noss,
Dave Foreman and John Terborgh in background
The Wildlands Project at work in Tucson, mid-to-late-1990s © Reed Noss

Dave Foreman: Advocate for the Big Wild

George Wuerthner

I remember the exact time and day I met Dave Foreman. It was 8:06 AM on October 28, 1983.

I was going to grad school at Montana State University in Bozeman, Montana. Dave and Howie Wolke were sleeping on the floor of my home. Howie and Dave were on a road trip to promote Earth First!. They didn't have much money and needed a place to sleep. So, I invited them to stay at my place in Bozeman. They arrived late at night, and I was already in bed. They made themselves comfortable by laying out sleeping pads and bags on the living room floor and were soon asleep.

In the morning, I was in the kitchen trying to be quiet as I made some coffee when Dave, still asleep on the floor, startled, suddenly bolted upright. He asked me if there was a freight train track next to the house. And as he asked the question, coffee was shaken from the cup I had just poured myself, and I noticed the light overhead was swaying.

What Dave felt and what shook my coffee cup was the 1983 Challis Idaho Earthquake, which registered 6.9 on the Richter Scale. Challis is nearly 300 miles from Bozeman, but the quake was strong enough to move the house and shake Dave awake.

So, my first meeting with Dave Foreman was announced by a natural event—a strong quake, an appropriate way to meet one of the most dedicated and staunch advocates for the Earth. He was like a walking Earthquake, and wherever Dave spoke, it was like having a quake right in the room. He got everyone's attention. People did not sleep through a Dave Foreman talk.

He could roar like a lion, but in private, he was like a kitten devoted to his wife, Nancy Morton.

He had a mischievous smile and laugh. He could be self-deprecating. He was a fantastic storyteller.

After that initial meeting, I had many subsequent encounters with Dave over the years. Starting in 1991, he and I, among others, including conservation biologists like Reed Noss and Michael Soulé, as well as wildlands activists like myself, were invited to North Face founder Doug Tompkins's home in San Francisco to discuss a way to promote more wildlands protections in the United States.

Tompkins wanted to create an organization that would think big and present persuasive science and philosophically based arguments for a continental-wide wildlands network. (Doug put these ideas to work by buying property in Patagonia and creating numerous national parks.)

At that meeting, and with Doug's financial assistance, we created The Wildlands Project to promote continent-wide conservation strategies and projects. I served on the Board for about a decade while Dave served as President of the Board. He had a natural leadership quality. People always deferred to him, not because he grabbed attention but because he always had well-thought-out ideas that he articulated well.

For much of the 1990s, Dave was the front man for The Wildlands Project, giving numerous interviews and speaking at conference events to promote the main idea that we needed a new approach to conservation—one that recognized that significant, connected wildlands were the only way to preserve biodiversity and stop the extinction of species.

Where Dave spoke someplace, you could bet there would be a crowd. I watched him numerous times enter an auditorium and capture the audience. He usually ended his talk with a group howl, which was cathartic for everyone.

Dave had an infectious sense of humor. Sitting around a campfire, swapping tales and adventures, you could hear him roar with laughter and mirth as he told another funny anecdote.

He was very fond of the Southwest wildlands. He particularly loved the Gila Wilderness, the Sky Islands, and the vastness of the Mexican-Arizona borderlands near the head of the Sea of Cortez.

Dave wasn't a scientist, but he was an avid naturalist. A voracious reader, the bookshelves in his home in Albuquerque covered the sweep and breadth of natural history, conservation history, and conservation science. He was a life-long student of the natural world and conservation politics. Dave's brilliance was his ability to synthesize those books, particularly conservation science, and present the main themes in a way ordinary people could understand.

He founded The Rewilding Institute, where he continued to advocate for large, connected wildland protection. From that perch, he expounded in his "Around the Campfire," begun in the *EF! Journal* and continued in *Wild Earth*, on all kinds of conservation issues and themes. Dave didn't shy away from controversy. He was an intellectually honest person.

It was disheartening to hear how he slipped on the stairs at Doug Tompkins's home on Renihue Fiord in Patagonia. The wooden steps were very smooth, and Tompkins required all guests to take off their shoes. So, we usually wore socks. But unfortunately, I slipped on the stairs while visiting Doug several times. And Dave learned the hard way. Dave was coming down for breakfast one morning and fell, hitting his back on the stairs. For years after that event, he had repeated back troubles that plagued him for the rest of his life.

Every time I go to the Southwest, I think of two people who profoundly influenced my thinking about the natural world—Aldo Leopold and Dave Foreman. His voice, laughter, and smile are gone, but his legacy remains in several thoughtful books and how people think about the Big Wild.

George Wuerthner is an ecologist, former river ranger for the Alaska BLM, and backcountry ranger in the Gates of the Arctic National Park in Alaska. He has visited more than 400 designated Wilderness Areas and approximately 200 National Park units. A prolific author, he has published 38 books, including such titles as *California Wilderness Areas*; *Alaska's Mountain Ranges*; *Nevada Mountain Ranges*; *Montana, Magnificent Wilderness*; *The Adirondacks: Forever Wild*; *Welfare Ranching: The Subsidized Destruction of the American West*; *Yellowstone: A Visitor's Companion*; *Protecting the Wild: Parks and Wilderness, Foundation for Conservation*; and *Wildfire: A Century of Failed Forest Policy.*

The Big Outside

Editor's Note: *The Big Outside*, researched and written by Dave and Howie Wolke, was published in 1989 and revised in 1992. It was the first comprehensive inventory of wild and roadless federal land in the United States since Bob Marshall's inventory in the mid-1930s. Marshall's "purpose was to draw attention to the vanishing universe of the wilderness and to encourage efforts toward the preservation of the largest and most important remnants of the American heritage." This, too, was the purpose of Dave and Howie's work.

The universe of the wilderness is disappearing
Like a snowbank on a south-facing
Slope on a warm June day.

– Robert Marshall

This book [*The Big Outside*] is a descriptive inventory of the remaining large roadless areas in the United States outside of Alaska and Hawaii: Every roadless area of 100,000 acres or larger in the Western states and 50,000 acres or larger in the Eastern states is listed and described, regardless of land ownership or administrative agency. It is as objective an inventory of the "Big Outside" as we, the authors, are capable of compiling.

It is also an argument for the idea of "Big Wilderness," for the notion that size is an important criterion for nature preserves. In other words, while protecting all remaining wildlands is important, protecting all remaining tracts of wild country is absolutely crucial.

We hope that by identifying the big areas that remain in an essentially roadless and undeveloped condition, we will be able to focus the attention of preservationists on them. The areas listed in this book are the most important wild areas in the United States. Conservation groups, individual activists, and conservation biologists should place a priority on these areas and defend them to the best of their abilities. In that sense, this book is a call to arms and a guidebook for action. Our research shows that there is a surprising number of large roadless areas left in many parts of the country, but a closer look reveals that these areas compose on a tiny fraction of the total acreage of temperate North America and are the paramount reservoirs of native diversity and ecological integrity in the United States.

This book is also a sad, lingering look at the vanishing American Wilderness. Many of these areas are under imminent threat of destruction from roading, logging, mining, grazing, and other abuses. In "The Destruction of Wilderness," we discuss the threats to wilderness in general, and in the remainder of the book, we tally the specific threats to each of the big roadless areas.

In the 1920s, Will Dilg, founder of the Izaak Walton League, wrote:

> *I am weary of civilization's madness and I yearn for the harmonious Gladness of the woods and of the streams. I am tired of your piles of Buildings and I ache from your iron streets. I feel jailed in your greatest Cities and I long for the unharnessed freedom of the big outside.*

The Big Outside is most especially an expression of our agreement with Dilg and of our absolute, fervid love for wilderness. We hope it will serve as a box of ammunition in the age-old struggle to defend the wild against those who "know the price of everything and the value of nothing."

– *The Big Outside*

Dave Foreman: Mentor

Jack Humphrey

I met Dave in Albuquerque in 1994.

My girlfriend, who was attending law school at the University of New Mexico, heard from a professor friend of Dave's that he and Nancy were living in Albuquerque. At the time I thought they lived in Tucson, so this came as a pleasant surprise. I asked my girlfriend to pass a note to her professor to pass to Dave.

At that point, I knew all the things about Dave that it was possible to know as an outsider and fan of his books. I'd just finished reading *The Big Outside*, and I was hooked. I just didn't know what to do with my desire to do conservation work. It was perhaps a week later that I got a call from him. I'd told him I was interested in getting into conservation work and would love to meet him sometime, to get his advice. His quick response was the first sign of his commitment to encouraging the next generation of conservationists. (Though I completely missed that part until many years later.) All I cared about was that I was meeting Dave Foreman! Founder of Earth First!. The guy who cracked Glen Canyon dam and ran around with Edward Abbey! We had lunch at a local restaurant on Coal Avenue by the university. It was the day that changed my path in life.

It wasn't until years later that I learned how generous Dave was with his time when it came to talking to young people about wilderness protection and rewilding. In fact, it wasn't until he left us, and the letters came pouring in from friends around the world, that I really got the picture. They each told stories of how they met Dave or were first inspired by him to go into careers they hadn't expected or to change majors midway through college. Dave had been recruiting and mentoring for a long time. Some people brought themselves into the movement after experiencing one of Dave's passionate son-of-a-preacher speeches about wild nature and the need to protect it. Others were encouraged by Dave personally after he spotted raw talent and an urgency to do something good.

Dave got me started by throwing me right into the lake to see if I could swim. One of the first wildlands network designs by the Wildlands Project was in the Sky Islands region of Southwest New Mexico, Southeast Arizona, and northern Sonora and Chihuahua Mexico. I became the executive director of Sky Island Alliance and raised money for the wildlands design workshops and field work. The work was important. Steep learning curve. And because Dave bought me lunch one day, I'd soon meet Michael Soulé at the first Sky Island mapping session. I also met Kim Crumbo and a host of other conservation legends and luminaries. I was in it for life at this point.

Organizer Dave opened doors for me professionally and exposed me to the upper ranks of the part of the conservation movement that I held in the highest regard. Professor Dave was always teaching. Often I'd come away from lunch at the Owl Cafe, his favorite spot, or from a visit to his house, with new facts about birds or some little-known history about Bob Marshall, Aldo Leopold, or Dave's early days at The Wilderness Society. He was always bursting with knowledge and love for nature, and he had to share it every chance he got, with whoever was around. And I tried to be around a lot.

You really can't talk about Dave Foreman without also talking about his wife, Nancy Morton. Individually they were forces of nature. Together, they were an indomitable conservation power couple. So much history. So much adventure. Dave and Nancy taught me everything about the highest form of exploration: river running. Nancy taught me everything I know about being a good river captain (tough, fair, fun), as well as river safety, planning, and navigation. And Dave became, well, *bigger* on the river. Everything about him was multiplied tenfold once he dropped an oar in the water. I will never forget how hard I laughed when Susan Morgan, a long-time friend from The Wilderness Society days in the 70's, once referred to Dave as "Himself." As in "Have you seen Himself today?" And Dave was never more Himself, in my experience, than when he was floating through hot, sandy, billion-year-old cracks in the desert.

The other place Dave was more Himself was on the trail. He and Nancy took us to the heart of one of Dave's favorite places on Earth, The Gila Wilderness. In his fifties, he made it a point to leave everyone in the dust on the trail. On that trip, I remember his pride in his mentee as I correctly identified a bear wallow and tracks in McKenna Park, the holiest of places in the Southwest.

Once Dave conducted a test of my ability to speak and do crowd work at a Wilderness conference in Albuquerque. My task was to present the Sky Island Wildland Network maps and findings to a friendly crowd. No one will ever know if I might have pulled off the presentation of a lifetime that day because Dave decided to sit in the front row, three feet away from me, smiling like a proud papa. I'm sure it was mostly for support, but Dave could also be ornery. We never talked about it, but he must have known the pressure it would put on me to present in front of one of the best speechifiers the conservation world had ever witnessed. I flopped so gloriously that Dave had to get up and fill in some blanks so that the attendees weren't left completely clueless. At one point I was talking but had no idea the words I was saying. I would not follow in Dave's footsteps as a great orator, but he continued to support me.

I got him back, though. I remember staying up all night with Dave and notorious cowboy poet Drum Hadley on his 300,000-acre ranch in the bootheel of New Mexico. Partying with Drum meant listening to his latest poems about being a gaucho in Mexico, drinking 32-year-old scotch, and throwing the bottles in the air while shooting pistols roughly in their direction. I finally retreated to my room around 4 am. The next morning Dave gave me hell about abandoning him with Drum, who made him stay up two more hours, drinking enough scotch to risk permanent blindness. I felt vindicated. The sting of my embarrassing flop at the wilderness conference softened as I pictured Dave trying to keep up with Hadley for what must have seemed a bank-busting Colorado River of single malt.

Dave taught me his strategy behind carefully maintaining a public image. I remember the things I knew about Dave before I met him: he was tough, a redneck for Wilderness, the first guy you'd want by your side in a bar brawl in Silver City. (Back when Silver City was full of wolf-hating ranchers and nary a *Subaru* in sight.) I always pictured Dave when I thought of Hayduke in Ed Abbey's *Monkey Wrench Gang*.

Then I visited him at his home in Albuquerque. That's when I met the whole Dave Foreman. In one afternoon, he went from a one-dimensional fictional character to a complicated, unexpected human being. No six-packs of cheap beer. No blue Jeep full of monkeywrenching gear in the driveway. I met a cat-loving, wine-sipping, birdwatcher!

I would come to know him as a man who was the greatest conservation historian I'd ever meet. And someone driven by a desire to soak up everything he could about nature and its wildeors. It would be almost two decades after we met before I saw a personal conservation library bigger and better than Dave's. I remember spending hours poring through coffee table books about endangered species as well as the classic and contemporary works of, well, everyone who'd written fact, fiction, song, or poem about nature.

I left Dave's house that evening with a picture of a far more multidimensional guy than his public persona. I'd met the man beyond the cover story, a highly intelligent and passionate defender of nature and a funny, sometimes hot-tempered person with flaws like the rest of us.

After meeting, interviewing, and becoming friends with a handful of Dave's *oldest compadres* over the years, I've come to know and highly respect Dave Foreman the man and conservationist. I'd used the word "hero" incorrectly several times in my life before meeting Dave. He defines that stature for me in many ways.

Today I picture Dave and Nancy paddling their own version of the Noatak. Youth restored, Dave can now easily outrun the Musk Ox that nearly trampled him there years ago. Though we are left to carry on Dave's work without him, he left behind a mountain of strategy, scholarship, and inspiration. He taught me that the work is never done, but to take the time to love it, to get out there and love wilderness for mental and physical health, and to stay focused on the prize. Give everything for the wildeors and give hell to anyone who gets in the way of protecting and restoring their homes.

Jack Humphrey started his conservation career in 1991 at the Washington, DC, Greenpeace office. In 1993, he moved to Chicago and became Canvas Director for Citizens for a Better Environment. In 1994, he moved to Albuquerque, New Mexico, met Dave Foreman, and the rest is history. As Executive Director of Sky Island Alliance,

Jack helped to organize one of the first published Wildlands Network Designs in partnership with The Wildlands Project.

Jack is a founding board member of the New Mexico Wilderness Alliance (now NM Wild). In the early 2000s, The Rewilding Institute was founded by Dave Foreman, and Jack has been the tech and marketing support behind rewilding.org and *Rewilding Earth* ever since.

Today he is the host of the *Rewilding Earth Podcast* and continues to support the spread of rewilding news, philosophy, and science as the Director of Digital Outreach for The Rewilding Institute.

Dave and Sam Hitt, White Rock Canyon © Dave Foreman Collection

A Giant in the Struggle

Sam Hitt

On Dave's first visit, he avoided our front door and came around the side, passing between our neighbor's dilapidated hog pen and the cold frames where tomato seedlings were being hardened off for later planting. It must have been spring sometime in the late 1970s. We knew we were about to receive a visitor because the hogs always grunted when someone came around that way.

Without officially introducing himself, Dave told me to forget the tomatoes. You can't grow tomatoes at 8,000 feet in the southern Rockies. Stick with hogs, he instructed, they eat anything and don't mind the cold winters. Only then did he reach out his hand and smile. "I've heard about you crazy hippies and thought I'd stop by to give you folks some advice!"

He had actually driven from his place in the Gila to our place near the Colorado border. The tomatoes were indeed an experiment in homesteading. I had studied agriculture in California and thought these determinate varieties might have a chance in our short growing season.

Dave made the trip at the suggestion of his neighbor, the late Bob Langsenkamp, who was helping Dave organize support for the Chama Canyon Wilderness Bill. Bob had visited a few months earlier, scouting for some redneck rural supporters. I had spent a couple of years in the Chama Canyon and told him about a crazy plan to dam the canyon to create a pump/storage electrical generating scheme. Turns out Bob knew about it and was as worried as I was.

When we invited Dave in for a cup of coffee, he immediately went to our dusty bookshelf. "Lookie here, *Deserts on the March* by the great Paul Sears." He then picked up *The Subversive Science* and read aloud from Starker Leopold's forward ("It's pretty obvious that industrialization is not of itself a panacea for man's woes."). I soon got the impression that we had passed some kind of test.

I'd bump into Dave over the years, at Earth First! rendezvous and various events. He kindly attended my farewell party when I left Forest Guardians after the old-growth wars in New Mexico had died down. He'd always ask about the tomatoes. In fact, after much trial and error, I did find a few tomato varieties that managed to produce ripe tomatoes before those early frosts. Being a carnivore guy, this would always amaze him.

Dave embodied the practical skills of organizing, thought leadership, and a gritty hope that kept us moving forward. Once the canyon was designated Wilderness, he inspired us to be more than defenders, to mold entire landscapes into a vision of wildness that seemed impossible to his clever critics and a host of well-meaning compromisers.

It was simply a matter of persuading enough folks with incisive critique, good stories, and humor that the impossible is really possible. This giant in the struggle for planetary life will be missed.

Sam Hitt has been active in conservation issues in the Southwest for nearly 40 years. He founded Elk Mountain Action in the early

1980s to protect old-growth forests, and in 1989 he founded Forest Guardians (now WildEarth Guardians). He is currently the founder and director of Wild Watershed, a volunteer group working on aquatic conservation in the Southwest. Sam serves as president of the Santa Fe Forest Coalition. Wild Watershed is a member group.

Honoring a Big Thinker

Brian Miller

I'm not sure that words are adequate to describe Dave. He often seemed larger than life, particularly when speaking to a crowd. His style was that of a preacher in an old-time tent revival. He was a commanding presence with his ability to speak, tell stories, and unmatched knowledge of conservation. The latter included important historical advances and analyses of present-day situations. He cut to the point and didn't sugarcoat his message. Shedding light is important. Ignorance and denial make dangerous policy. For this unsparing analysis, the *Wall Street Journal* crowd disliked him, and big foundations squirmed when he called out their predilection for fundraising instead of action. His dedication to conservation was as passionate and sincere as anyone I have known. That passion, dedication, and relentless pursuit of protecting nature has stimulated many others into action and helped make the world a better place.

Perhaps one of his greatest contributions was pushing conservationists to think bigger than local efforts. He didn't disparage local efforts and indeed kept his yard a haven for birds and insects. But successful conservation needs a much larger scale of thought. The Wildlands Project, a group Dave co-founded, pushed landscape-level action involving a series of core protected areas linked by corridors. In the west, that meant from Mexico to the Yukon along the Rocky Mountain spine of the continent. Dave wrote the first Wildlands Vison (landscape plan) and it covered the Sky Islands. He also co-authored the Southern Rockies Ecosystem Vision and encouraged others in the conservation community to do the same in their regions.

Some large, mainstream NGOs balked at this idea because "it would scare people away from conservation." Now, those same organizations have departments for landscape conservation. One of the early mottos of The Wildlands Project was "steal this idea." It worked. The Wildlands Project did not want to be a typical NGO. The plan of the original Board was that when large-scale conservation became accepted, the organization would disband. There was no need for an endowment. The mission was purely conservation, not organizational perpetuation.

The Wildlands Project also pushed the importance of carnivores and other keystone species. Such species regulate ecosystem function and provide evolutionary potential. The emphasis on large carnivores promoted the value of these creatures to functional nature. Previously, many thought that productivity drove systems from the bottom-up. Thus, carnivores sat at the top of the food chain, taking prey but not giving anything back. But we now know that carnivores, in their act of predation, regulate ecosystems from the top-down. When carnivores are removed from a system, herbivores explode in number, and that decimates the plant community.

Yet, these magnificent animals are still persecuted. Perhaps keystone species are persecuted so heavily because they push a system toward complexity and resilience through their actions. But for humans to profit economically, they need to simplify a system to control it. Simplification, however, breaks the numerous and complex linkages of nature, making the few remaining links more vulnerable to catastrophe and collapse. As Aldo Leopold pointed out, we lack a land ethic that includes nature in our global community. When decisions are made based on economic profit, nature only gets what is left over. For too long, humans have abused the land because it is viewed as an economic commodity. To our national shame, greed drove decisions. Dave coined the term "rewilding" as a method of combating human greed and restoring wilderness as self-willed land.

I was fortunate enough to meet him when I joined the Board of the old Wildlands Project. That was in 1993 when I was living and working in Mexico. What started as a working relationship grew into friendship. Dave had a soft side and a wonderful sense of humor. He once told me that his public persona was not who he really was down deep. But that public persona was pure genius and served nature well. He once told me that he dressed as a cowboy and went to a public meeting in Cody, WY, where they were complaining about grizzly bears and their effect on the ranching community. Dave stood in the back and listened. Toward the end of the meeting, Dave spoke. He said, "If you folks can't handle a bit of the old west because of your fear of grizzlies, then load them in a truck and bring them to New Mexico. We'll live with them." He said that people approached him afterward and apologized.

Dave was able to accomplish so much that many didn't know about his bouts with depression. Winston Churchill called depression "his black dog," and Dave adopted that term. We talked about that often, as I am also touched by it. He once joked that he was manic-depressive. He said that in his manic stage he started organizations, but that they conspired to give him medicine so that he won't start any more groups. Losing Nancy in January 2021 contributed to his depression. She was his rock. If you were lucky enough to ride a river with Nancy, it was clear that she was in charge of the whole operation.

Dave's loss is hard to comprehend. There is no doppelganger to step into his empty niche. For many of us, the loss is also personal. I was glad that I had a chance to tell him goodbye. He said that he had hoped to hang around and do more, but he had already done so much. I won't ever forget him. Kudos my friend. You live on in all of us. We will do our best to uphold your example.

Brian J. Miller received a Ph.D. from the University of Wyoming in behavioral ecology and conservation of black-footed ferrets and was then awarded a Smithsonian Institution Fellowship at their Conservation and Research Center. He worked with the conservation of the endangered black-footed ferret for a decade, then lived in Mexico for five years, beginning an ongoing research project on jaguars and pumas in the dry tropical forest of Jalisco, Mexico. After seven years as a Coordinator of Conservation and Research at the Denver Zoological Foundation, Brian accepted a position to develop conservation and education programs at the Wind River Foundation. His main research interest concerns the role of highly interactive species (keystones) in regulating ecosystem processes and how to improve protection for those species when designing reserves. He has published 200 scientific articles and seven books, and he has been on the board of five conservation organizations. He has helped start two protected areas, one of which is the Rio Mora National Wildlife Refuge. In 2009, he was given the Denver Zoo's Annual Conservation Award.

As one of Dave's closest confidants and collaborators, he trusted Brian for scientifically sound counsel and rock-solid advice to help with everything from conservation specifics to organizational program development.

Healing the Wounds: Goal-Setting

To rewild North America, we must have a vision that is bold, scientifically credible, practically achievable, and hopeful. The practically achievable part requires specific goals and action steps—organized to heal the specific wounds.

Although ecological restoration is essential for an overall conservation strategy, it is painfully clear that, in the twenty-first century, wildlands and wildlife will continue to be imperiled by human activities. A frontier approach to exploiting nature still rules in much of Canada, the United States, Mexico, and Central America. Restoration will come to naught if further wounding of the land is not stopped. Therefore, each of the seven healing-the-wounds goals is twofold: (1) to prevent additional wounding, and (2) to heal existing wounds. The following goals are adapted from the New Mexico Highlands Wildlands Network Vision.

Goal 1: Permanent protection of extant native species from extinction or endangerment, and recovery of all species native to the continent except those already extinct.

Goal 2: Permanent protection of all habitat types from further degradation and loss, and restoration of degraded habitats.

Goal 3: Protection of the land from further fragmentation, and restoration of functional connectivity for all species native to the region.

Goal 4: Restoration and permanent protection of the functioning of ecological and evolutional processes.

Goal 5: Prevention of the further spread of exotic species (including pathogens), and elimination or control of exotic species already present.

Goal 6: Prevention of the further introduction of ecologically harmful pollution into the region, and removal or containment of existing pollutants.

Goal 7: Management of landscapes and wildlife to provide opportunities for adaptation and adjustment to climate change.

These are heady goals. With nearly half a billion people living in North America (including Central America), they can be gained in the near term only in part or even in small part for much of the continent. They apply completely only to wildlands networks in regions still wild or suitable for major restoration.

Moreover, these goals are comprehensive and should be embraced in principle by the whole conservation movement and land managers. No one organization can tackle them all, but all who love nature should adopt them as overarching goals for twenty-first-century conservation. They must be carried out on local, regional, and continental scales.

– Dave Foreman
Rewilding North America,
A Vision for Conservation in the 21st Century
Chapter 7, Conservation Biology

Dave Foreman Shaped My Life as a Conservationist

Reed Noss

Dave Foreman was and is one of the major inspirations in my life and one of the greatest conservationists in the history of North America. It was sometime in 1981 when it all began for me. I was sitting in my windowless office at the Ohio Department of Natural Resources, bored as hell, thumbing through some early Earth First! newsletters (including Vol. 1, No. 1 from Nov. 1, 1980, edited by Dave Foreman and Howie Wolke), which some thoughtful friend had sent to me. I was enthralled with the wild ideas in those primitive hand-typed newsletters, particularly the call for massive ecological preserves—"the core of the EF! platform"—to represent all the nation's ecoregions. Living in the ecologically degraded southern Midwest near the edge of the Appalachians, I particularly appreciated this statement in Vol. 1, No. 1:

> Protection of some of our remaining wilderness is not enough. Protection of all of it is not enough. Not only does EARTH FIRST support wilderness designation for all Forest Service RARE II areas and BLM roadless areas, we also believe that in order to preserve the ecological integrity of our country, it is time to *recreate* wilderness: identify key areas, close roads, remove developments, and reintroduce extirpated wildlife.

Damn, those were powerful words, and I'm pretty sure they were Dave's (with no slight to Howie). They may represent one of his earliest published statements in support of rewilding, a term he coined in the early 1990s, which is now an international movement. Dave's words here echo a statement the great ecologist Victor Shelford, first president of the Ecological Society of America, made in a memo to his Preservation Committee in 1931: "There

John Davis, Dave, and Reed Noss, 1987 © Reed Noss
Very serious hikers

needs to be restoration of the primitive as well as protection of the primitive." Shelford got into some trouble with the Ecological Society board over his advocacy, and eventually his committees were disbanded. I suspect Shelford and Foreman would have been close comrades, had they not belonged to different generations.

I had been thinking along similar lines in the late 1970s and early 1980s and had argued for the enlargement of forest blocks and their connection by corridors in my 1979 master's thesis on birds of a southwestern Ohio nature reserve. Moreover, I was getting more and more fed up with the environmental community in Ohio, which seemed to lack vision and courage. I had been attending local Audubon, Sierra Club, and Friends of the Earth meetings, and virtually no one was interested in large-scale conservation—certainly not the leaders of these groups. Every action to protect Nature was being justified in terms of outdoor recreational opportunities or human health. Everyone seemed willing to compromise away the last wild spaces, so long as they could have a pleasant hike on the new boardwalk at the local park. No one was saying that wild things and wild places were valuable for their own sake and that it was ethically wrong to destroy them. No one was taking a hardline stand for the wild. No one was talking about recreating wilderness, something I desperately wanted to happen in Ohio. It had to happen!

Reading the early Earth First! newsletters, I realized I had finally found some like-minded people who were willing to take a stand for the wild. I wrote to the address on the newsletters and expressed my interest in becoming a contact in Ohio. Dave wrote me a wonderful letter in response (I wish I still had it) and my wife, Myra, and I soon formed an Ohio group (there was already an Ohio contact, but I couldn't seem to locate him). Frankly, we didn't get much accomplished, but we stirred up some of the local environmental meetings and drank a lot of beer.

In 1982, I began contributing articles to the *EF! Journal*. And in 1983, after moving to Florida, I aligned with Florida EF!, and we did get some things done. We stopped through direct action a couple of egregious developments in northern Florida (Myra and some others were arrested for tree-sitting on a development site on the edge of Paynes Prairie State Preserve), occupied and defiled the U.S. Forest Service office in Tallahassee over their continued logging of old-growth longleaf pines, and published a newsletter (*The Wiregrass*) that became very popular with the Florida environmental community, including within state agencies. Dave and Mike Roselle visited and gave inspiring and well-attended talks at the University of Florida, where I was a Ph.D. student. I was especially thrilled by Dave's fire-and-brimstone speaking style (something I would never even try to pull off myself). Our EF! group, by speaking and acting the truth about what was happening to Florida, was effectively shaming the big conservation groups, especially the very weak (at the time) Florida chapter of the Sierra Club, which bent over backward to compliment and compromise with the Forest Service and other federal and state agencies over just about everything.

In 1985, directly inspired by Dave's writings and speeches about recreating wilderness, I published an article in the *Earth First! Journal* that introduced what is probably the crowning achievement of my career thus far—the first rendition of the now widely popular and well-funded Florida Wildlife

Corridor, which at the time I called a "wilderness recovery" plan. No other outlet would have published such a paper in the 1980s. I got death threats by phone after publicizing the plan at environmental conferences (my corridor map appeared in newspapers statewide), and we couldn't let our daughter play in the front yard for fear of her safety. Yet, those days of ambitious and radical conservation were some of the most gratifying days of my environmental career. They were certainly the most invigorating. I owe it all to Dave Foreman and Earth First!.

I appreciate that some friends and colleagues of Dave's now want to draw attention away from his more radical and controversial days with Earth First! and focus on his later accomplishments. This is understandable. For years people have tried to tar Dave's reputation for his support for civil disobedience and especially for his enthusiastic advocacy of ecological sabotage ("monkey-wrenching"). When various anarchists, Marxists, and rebels without a cause took over Earth First! in 1990 (and stated in the journal that there would be "no more conservation biology" printed there), I left the group along with Dave, John Davis, and others. The following year we co-cofounded The Wildlands Project, along with Michael Soulé, Doug Tompkins, George Wuerthner, Mitch Friedman, David Johns, Jamie Sayen, Monte Hummel, and other committed wilderness defenders whose words had graced the *EF! Journal* for a decade. *Wild Earth*, the magazine closely associated with The Wildlands Project, with Dave as executive editor and John Davis and later Tom Butler as editors, reached a level of literary excellence that would never have been possible with the *EF! Journal.*

The Wildlands Project (later renamed Wildlands Network) and Dave's later co-creation, The Rewilding Institute, have done some wonderful things, and I support them wholeheartedly. But it's not quite the same as the old days. Maybe I'm getting too nostalgic, but I miss the energy and radicalism of the original Earth First!. Can we please try to recapture some of that excitement? The Earth desperately needs spirited and uncompromising defenders willing to raise hell (with a sense of humor, I might add). As for myself, I've become an establishment conservation scientist, and I work within the system, doing what I can (given those constraints) to protect and rewild the Earth. But the inspiration for all that I do comes largely from

Dave and others who had tried working within the system but were often at odds with that system because it was too bound by timidity and a desire to appear professional and reasonable.

Ironically, many of the ideas expressed in the EF! newsletters and journal from the very beginning—and seen as radical, hopelessly impractical, and even scary at the time—have become well accepted by conventional conservationists. These ideas include establishing large protected core areas to represent every ecoregion (as also proposed earlier by Shelford and his colleagues), connecting core areas by broad habitat corridors, closing and obliterating roads, reintroducing large carnivores, and other aspects of rewilding. These themes are now thoroughly embraced by the mainstream conservation community. Would this ever have happened without Dave Foreman and his EF! comrades vigorously demanding these actions long before they were popular? I doubt it. Conservationists of all stripes owe Dave a big debt of gratitude. And they should heed his call for a return to the idealistic first principles of conservation. As Dave stated in the *EF! Journal* 7(4) in 1987:

> Earth First! in many ways represents a fundamentalist revival within the wilderness/wildlife preservation movement, a return to basics, and a reaction against co-option and compromise. Over the last several decades as the conservation movement has grown in prominence, it has replaced Aldo Leopold's Land Ethic with political pragmatism, Bob Marshall's wilderness vision with modest reaction to government programs, John Muir's passion with an accountant's rationalism, and Henry David Thoreau's courage with a desire not to rock the boat. It was this essential corruption of the conservation movement's historical roots that brought forth Earth First! out of the mainstream of the movement. At the heart of our message is a return to ethics, vision, passion, and courage.

Reed Noss is a writer, photographer, lecturer, and consultant in natural history, ecology, and conservation. He serves as Chief Science Advisor for the Southeastern Grasslands Initiative and the Endangered

Ecosystems Alliance. He was formerly Provost's Distinguished Research Professor of Biology at the University of Central Florida. He received a B.S. in education from the University of Dayton, an M.S. in ecology from the University of Tennessee, and a Ph.D. in wildlife ecology from the University of Florida.

Reed served as Editor-in-Chief of *Conservation Biology*, Science Editor for *Wild Earth* magazine, and President of the Society for Conservation Biology. He is an Elected Fellow of the American Association for the Advancement of Science.

I Think Mother Nature Was Crying...

Bob Howard

I was at Dave's home when he died. The following day I drove home alone along a rural route that we had both traveled extensively and arrived home safely in Silver City. The drive had Aldo Leopold, Gila, and Blue Wilderness to my sides and in front of me. West on US 60, turn SW at Datil through Reserve, then South on US 189 through Glenwood, where Debby used to tend bar, and Pleasanton, where Dave and Debby lived in the early 1970s. The area was greener than I can ever recall, and both the Plains of San Augustine and the many mountains were gorgeous. The sky varied from full sun through partial clouds to full overcast, then sprinkles of rain starting at the Continental Divide and torrential rain just north of Glenwood. I think Mother Nature was crying...

Bob (Robert E.) Howard, M.D., Ph.D., is a retired medical school professor, retired consultant, and fifty-year environmental activist. He held many and varied leadership positions in the Sierra Club, at local, state, regional, national, and international levels. Perhaps the most important were serving as Vice President for Planning for over a decade and serving on the national Board of Directors for four years as Vice President (with conservation oversight) and two years as Treasurer. At home in New Mexico, Bob works primarily on Wilderness designation and protection.

Dave Foreman, Stuart Pimm, and Michael Soulé brainstorming how best to thwart the Forces of Darkness who would damage Earth and exterminate its species. © *Stuart Pimm*

To Dave

Susie O'Keeffe

We have only met a few times, but I would like to tell you a story to remind you how many souls you have touched and inspired to love and fight for the wild ones and the world.

I was a young woman, probably twenty-five years old when I first heard you talk. My best friend, Jenn Carroll Wilson, and I were working for Huey Johnson in San Francisco. Jenn and I would run off into the Sierras together to backpack every chance we got. We were learning how to be out there, and often we would get lost, get soaked in the rain, or be devoured by mosquitoes. She was my first truly "wild" friend. And, as she said, we found "God in those mountains." She taught me to backcountry ski, use a map and compass, and opened my passion for all the wild ones. When you came to talk at Fort

Mason, she insisted we go. You bellowed and howled, you brought the souls of the animals into the room, and the truth that all the wild beings and forces had the right to be free and thrive in our hearts. Your raw, pure, honest, and fearless love gave us permission to love what we loved. You made us laugh; you made us cry. We left utterly and permanently transformed and empowered. We often recalled that day with laughter and joy. It was the day the direction of our lives was determined.

I know the heartbreak for our wild kin tears into all of us each day. I wish you peace from that sadness now, Dave. May you pass over with ease, knowing that you did all that you possibly could for them. May everything you fought for so beautifully and honestly greet you in all the glory that is Wild. Nancy is there, waiting...

With deep, deep gratitude,
Susie

Susie O'Keeffe lives at the headwaters of the Sheepscot River in Maine. She is the Board Vice President of Northeast Wilderness Trust and a board member of Upstream Watch. She holds a Master's with distinction from Oxford University in Environmental Management and is a research associate at the College of the Atlantic.

Continue to Think Big, Be Bold, Push Boundaries, and Save the Wild...

Kathleen H. Fitzgerald

Biliquo Bulesa Conservancy is in Isiolo County, northern Kenya. Its southern boundary is the Ewaso Nyiro River, which originates on Mt. Kenya. Remote, dry, and difficult to get to, the conservancy is 377,300 hectares, comprised mainly of acacia scrub and Doum palms. The area is riddled with insecurity and cattle raiding. I was camping there in February 2022. It was 42 degrees Celsius, sweltering hot. We scouted elephants, hippos, birds, and other species on foot early in the morning and late evenings when the sun was slightly forgiving. Midday we lay in the muddy river keeping watch for crocodile.

One evening, our host emerged from his tent in a crisp, short-sleeved white Earth First! t-shirt. He said he was fed up with ecological destruction and it was time to put the Earth first. I had been living in Africa for 15 years and was always amazed that very few people had heard of some of the great conservationists of North America, and yet here, in the middle of the bush, in a very remote location, Dave Foreman was the topic of discussion.

Under the brilliant stars that evening I thought about Dave's vast reach. When I returned home to Ol Pejeta Conservancy, I emailed Dave, copying some close friends, and recounted the story. I thanked him for his great influence and deep legacy. I think he enjoyed the tale. He offered to send me one of the original Earth First! t-shirts he still had stashed in his home and indicated that he wanted to visit Africa again to go birding, perhaps Botswana, he said.

I met Dave almost thirty years prior to that camping trip. In 1991, I was a university student in upstate New York. I read Christopher Manes' book *Green Rage* and marched into my advisor's office, proclaiming that I wanted to

L to R, Standing, Unidentified, Ken Sanders, Howie Wolke, Clarke Abbey, Jack Loeffler, Bob Greenspan, Dave Peterson, kneeling, Bart Koehler, sitting, Katie Lee, John Nichols, Dave Foreman, Celebrating Ed Abbey at the Pack Creek Ranch, Moab, Utah, 2004 © Dave Foreman Collection

cement my feet into roads to block the development that was destroying our natural heritage. He shook his head and with a slight smirk, sent me down the street to the *Wild Earth* office. After meeting John Davis, Mary Davis, and eventually Tom Butler, I started working at *Wild Earth* and later The Wildlands Project. Dave was the editor at the time and had recently launched The Wildlands Project with Reed Noss, Michael Soulé, Doug Tompkins, and other pioneers.

Strategic and bold, Dave changed the conservation movement. He pushed boundaries that needed to be pushed. He was not afraid to say what needed to be said. He made people feel uncomfortable when needed. He spoke for the unspoken and inspired others to find their voice. He helped me find my voice.

Dave was way ahead of his time. At The Wildlands Project, we drew big lines on maps in the early 1990s—cores, corridors, and buffers—that were considered radical then. Now, they form the blueprints for conservation planning. Dave spoke decades ago about the need to factor in the cost of nature into our accounting systems. Today, natural capital accounting is finally catching on, and the world is slowly realizing that we rely on nature and it is not free.

Dave inspired people with his vision and created space for people to think big. His wolf howl conjured up the wild in any auditorium and ignited what he called the "fire in your belly." People flocked to hear him. He must have given hundreds of talks, inspiring thousands of people to get involved in nature conservation. In 1994, we organized a speaking event with Dave and David Brower at the Ethan Allen chapel on the University of Vermont campus in Burlington, Vermont. Thousands of people came to hear these two conservation giants. Many people at the chapel that cool evening left with renewed or a new commitment to conservation. What an incredible legacy.

As a young conservationist, spending time in the wilderness with Dave, his wife Nancy Morton, and other *Wild Earth* colleagues was a thrill. We had memorable adventures canoeing in the Adirondack Park's Five Ponds Wilderness, bushwacking to find remnant old-growth trees, and camping in Cabeza Prieta National Wildlife Refuge. We shared many magical nights around the campfire debating how best to save nature.

It has been thirty years since a small group of us produced, labeled, and lugged large grey sacks of *Wild Earth* magazine to the post office in Canton, New York. During that period, the ecological fabric of our planet has unwound. We have lost half of the population of the African lion. The African elephant faced a severe poaching crisis, less than 25,000 black and white rhinos are left in the wild, and habitat across Africa has been decimated. Coupled with the current and projected impacts of climate change, the outlook is bleak. However, there are many hopeful examples of conservation wins.

Gorongosa National Park in Mozambique, for example, was leveled during the Civil War. Today, despite ongoing conflict in the country and a challenging work environment, it has thriving wildlife populations and is strongly supported by local communities who benefit from jobs and rural development programs. Gonarezhou National Park in Zimbabwe and Liuwa Plains National Park in Zambia have similar stories of ecological, social, and economic recovery. The population increase of the mountain gorilla in Uganda,

Rwanda, and the Democratic Republic of Congo from 254 in 1981 to 1063 in 2019 is perhaps one of the most remarkable recovery stories given the regional conflict and the need to work across three complex countries. Each of these cases is the result of vision, persistence, passion, and boldness—traits that Dave embodied. They are also solid examples of recovery.

In December 2022, almost every country in the world signed the Kunming-Montreal Agreement, at the heart of which is a commitment to protect at least 30% of the world's lands and oceans by 2030. This is the most significant global commitment ever made to biodiversity conservation. Currently, only 17% of terrestrial areas and 10% of marine areas globally are protected. The agreement also recognizes the important role and leadership of Indigenous Peoples and local communities. According to the Campaign for Nature, "now the critical work begins to ensure that important areas for biodiversity are prioritized and that the systems of conserved areas are well connected and representative of the world's diverse ecosystems." Many of these seeds were planted decades ago.

The best way to honor Dave is to carry on his work. To continue to think big, be bold, push boundaries, and save the wild. That's my plan.

Kathleen H. Fitzgerald is a protected area specialist with over two decades of experience in integrated large landscape conservation and development programs in Africa and North America. Kathleen has worked in 19 countries. She created new conservation and protected areas (CPA), improved management and financial sustainability of CPAs, established Collaborative Management Partnerships for PA management in six countries covering 14 million acres, and led community and climate resiliency initiatives. She has developed REDD+ projects, biodiversity offsets, and impact bonds. She was Vice President at the African Wildlife Foundation and a partner at Conservation Capital and is the Senior Manager of the Global Project for Permanence Initiative at Pew Charitable Trusts, a Senior Advisor to the World Bank's Global Wildlife Program, and a member of the World Commission on Protected Areas Advisory Group.

Population: The Toughest Issue

Dave was convinced that unless the United States and the rest of the world faced up to the problem of overpopulation, the efforts of conservationists to protect wilderness and wildlife, and to rewild, would be impossible. He was very frustrated that powerful conservationists and conservation organizations shied away from the issue, deeming it too controversial. He did not shy away from it¬—in fact, he wrote a book about it and got into trouble with some who considered him misanthropic and anti-modern. Dave never minced words and was proud that he stood against the ideology of endless growth, whether it be of the human population or the economy. Such growth, he knew, was unsustainable and ultimately impossible. A finite planet could not support human society based on infinite growth. Here is an excerpt from *Man Swarm* that summed up his position on this issue:

> The big question for lovers of wild things is the one that Garrett Hardin threw at us in 1972. "[H]ow do we get the general body politic to accept the truth?" Today, though, we must first ask, "How do we get conservationists and environmentalists to accept the truth?" In my worst nightmares, I never thought we'd come to this sad day when my own gang wimped out on the underlying threat: The unending rampage of topsy-turvy growth.
>
> Over the last two hundred years, some of the world's most farsighted thinkers have warned about human overpopulation. If we look at the warp and woof of their writings,

> we can tease out five threads of population-growth outcomes: (1) hunger and starvation because we can't grow enough to feed ourselves; (2) squandering natural resources (raw goods) until we run out; (3) landscalping and the loss of land fertility; (4) cultural, economic, and political upheaval; and (5) harm to wild things. Most limits-to-growth seers have worried most about the first four—after all, they are about us. Far fewer have given heed to how our growth gobbles up wild neighborhoods and pulls the extinction-trigger at a swelling stream of species each year—soon to be an overwhelming flood. As a lover of wild things, my worry has always been about how our growth bashes all the other Earthlings.

Dave was not naïve. He understood too well the difficulties those who would raise this issue would face, yet he did not despair. He knew what measures would be necessary and listed some of them in *Man Swarm*. He knew too the deep-seated cultural obstacles to necessary change and also what the outcome would be if change did not happen. He wrote, "What we do or don't do today will build the world of tomorrow." That is an inescapable truth!

A Person of Conscience and a Force for Consciousness

Warren Hern

My first knowledge of Dave Foreman was when I discovered somehow that he had included an abstract of my 1990 paper, "Why are there so many of us? Description and diagnosis of a planetary ecopathological process" in his compendium, *Books of the Big Outside* (Fall, 1991). I think I had heard his name, but I didn't know who he was. When I found a copy of this publication, I was astounded by the breadth and depth of the annotated bibliography contained in this collection, which included works by ecological historian Alfred Crosby and population expert William Catton, both of whom I knew personally and whose work was among the best. The entire collection of *Books of the Big Outside* was and remains the best introduction to the literature on natural history and environmental conservation I have seen. It is an invaluable resource. It clearly was assembled by someone—Dave Foreman—who had a keen eye for the essential materials and a broad vision of the struggle to save the world ecosystem in which we must survive. The selection had a moral fervor to it. It is an invaluable reference for me.

It was my great honor to have my first journal publication on this subject included in Dave's collection. "Who the hell is this guy?" I thought. "I must find him and meet him." I had heard about Earth First! and Dave, then I realized the connection.

At about that time, I was invited to a social event at the home of environmental leader friends in Colorado, Bill and Louise Mounsey, where I met Dave for the first time as well as saw some old friends with whom I had been out in the Colorado wilderness (including John Peleaux, who taught me winter camping and how to make a snow cave).

Dave and I hit it off. From there, he quoted my work in several other venues, and I went to hear him speak at the Boulder Book Store, where they had a book event for his book, *Man Swarm and the Killing of Wildlife* (2011). He signed my copy of his book. Unfortunately, that was the last time I saw him.

Dave was intrigued by my idea that the human species has become a malignant process on the planet. He had a somewhat different idea, but we were on the same page. I was intrigued by his idea of rewilding, with which I agreed, but I was not optimistic that this good idea was feasible because it is the antithesis of modern society. It was also supported by my friend Paul Martin, the astute paleopalynologist who developed the "overkill" hypothesis that explained the sudden extinction of many North American megafauna within a very short time after the entrance of the Pleistocene hunters into North America. Paul vigorously supported the idea of rewilding. Modern humans regard wildlife as pests to be exterminated. Look at the assassinations of re-introduced wolves in Yellowstone.

Dave Foreman was first a person of conscience and also a force for consciousness of what we are doing as a species to our home, the Earth. He was a force for a moral imperative to understand and value the natural world from whence we came and in which we live. He was a force for a moral imperative to act to save and protect the beauty and value of other beings with whom we share the planet, whether they are human or not.

In my analysis, the human species is not just a "man swarm" as Dave has characterized it, and not just a superficial "dermatitis" on the Earth, as others have said, but a truly malignant process on the planet. We have become a superorganism, a new species that I call *Homo ecophagus*—"the man who devours the ecosystem." This new species—of which we are all part—is engaged in the process of converting all plant, animal, organic, and inorganic material on the planet into human biomass and its adaptive adjuncts and support systems. Since it is malignant, it is a terminal process, and it is at a very advanced stage, in my opinion. Earth First! was a strong reaction to this, and Dave's leadership with this and The Rewilding Institute are visible and tangible efforts to stop or reverse this process. The Rewilding Institute is an especially positive step toward allowing other species to exist in the natural environment and ecosystems that have been under destruction by humans to the detriment of all.

Dave's message is particularly urgent and pertinent now, as each day's headlines tell us of both ecological catastrophes happening now and those that are about to happen. Each day brings news of threats to more of the irreplaceable species with whom we share the Earth. Each day tells us more emphatically that we must stop and reverse this destruction. We must understand that we humans are among the most destructive forces to hit the planet, but we can change that if we listen to people like Dave.

Dave's death makes me very sad. He was one of the true souls who understood both our moral dilemma and the threat to our own survival because we don't care enough about the other species—plant and animal—that inhabit the Earth that we share. Dave was angry about the destruction we have wrought on the Earth and our collective resistance to stopping this madness. His anger and creative response to this global challenge inspired me, as it has inspired others. It's worth being mad about. His death is a great loss. I miss him. The world is less without him.

Warren M. Hern is a Colorado physician specializing in women's health care who is also the co-founder and chairman of the Holy Cross Wilderness Defense Fund. He is the author of *Homo Ecophagus: A Deep Diagnosis to Save the Earth* (Routledge, 2022).

He Spoke for the Wild World

Karen Shragg

To understand my deep admiration for the late, great Dave Foreman, one only has to look at the subtitle for the second edition of his book *Man Swarm: How Overpopulation is Killing the Wild World* (2014). He could have picked anything to address—human sanity, overcrowded cities, homelessness—but he chose the wild world. Dave Foreman was the 'Lorax' who spoke for the trees and devoted his life to making room for them. As a lifelong naturalist, writer, and nature center director, I share his motivation to represent the well-being of all wild things, but I can only hope to have his impact.

It's hard to say what I admired most about Dave: his books, his willingness to be arrested for his beliefs, his ability to start conservation organizations and then leave them when they started to go off the rails? Yes, to all of that and more, but at the center of it all was his unwillingness to compromise the integrity of wildlands for the current political weather. He focused on the issues that would help protect his beloved wildlands the most, including overpopulation and all of the ways it happens. Fearless to discuss immigration policy with a practical voice, he began fighting this contentious issue we are still contending with years ago when he said, "I strenuously reject the idea that any and all ecologically-grounded concerns about human overpopulation are racist and fascist."

He always kept wildlands in the bullseye of his efforts and paved the way for more of us to do the same. Dave tried to pry us loose from the chains of anthropocentrism, which is ultimately going to harm us, and he made a strong case throughout his career that we need wildlands in both physical and psychological ways. Dave never succumbed to his critics because he knew that the future of wolves, bears, mountain lions, and their ilk was more important than the short-term interests of those oblivious to their beauty and value.

I will forever rest my head on the mantra, WWDD, "What Would Dave Do?" when it comes to my own activism on overpopulation, because the answer is clear: He would keep his eye on the prize and just keep on fighting, and that, my friends and colleagues, is the best way we could honor this legendary wildlife hero.

Karen Shragg is a lifelong environmentalist, naturalist, educator, poet, author, and overpopulation activist. She received her doctorate from the University of St. Thomas in 2002, following two other degrees in education. She retired as a long-time naturalist and nature center director to start the LLC, Move Upstream Environmental Consulting (MUSEC). In 2015, her book *Move Upstream, A Call for Overpopulation*, was published by Freethought House Press. Her newest book moves the discussion further upstream. *Change Our Stories, Change Our World* was published in November 2020, by the same press.

Karen is a board member of SEPS (Scientists and Environmentalists for Population Stabilization) and serves on the board of Californians for Population Stabilization. She also served on the advisory board of World Population Balance from 1992 to 2021.

The Rewilding Institute

Dave left The Wildlands Project in 2003, which continues its important work to this day. He moved on to another phase in which his emphasis was on thinking and writing, what might be called his scholarly period. A gifted and hard-working writer, he had many ideas to explore, foremost among them rewilding. What would it take to rewild North America, for instance? To facilitate this stage of his work, he formed The Rewilding Institute (TRI), inviting a small group of colleagues to join him in defining rewilding and exploring what would be necessary to achieve it. He declared TRI a "think tank" and his comrades in the thinking were to be "fellows," though not all his female compatriots were enamored of this title.

At this stage, Dave was hobbled by health problems, principally pain resulting from a fall that damaged vertebrae and required surgeries. He had, in addition, struggled with depression throughout his life, and his physical difficulties and the resultant medications exacerbated his ups and downs. His body might not be working as it had and as he would like, but his mind was as sharp as ever. He would forge ahead with the tools and strength he had, and he entered a very productive phase, writing five books over the next fifteen years. He wrote his popular column "Around the Campfire" in *Wild Earth* until the journal ceased publication, then posted it on The Rewilding Institute website, *Rewilding Earth* (rewilding.org).

Early in this phase, his principal effort went into a book project that would ultimately be titled *Rewilding North America: A Vision for Conservation in the 21st Century*, and it would be considered by many to be his *magnum opus*. He poured his studies of environmental crisis into it, summarizing "forty-thousand years of extinction in North America" and recent problems like habitat loss and fragmentation, degradation of ecological processes, and climate change, among others. He then gave an overview of "new conservation," particularly key insights from conservation biology and the work that he and others had been doing with The Wildlands Project and were advocating under the banner of The Rewilding Institute. Finally, he presented his grand vision for a North American Network being addressed by The Wildlands Project, which became The Wildlands Network, and summarized what land management forms would be necessary to achieve this vision. The book was published by Island Press.

While doing the research and writing on *Rewilding North America*, affectionately known to his friends as *RNA*, he indulged another of his dreams, to write fiction. He wrote *The Lobo Outback Funeral Home*, a novel published by the University Press of Colorado in 2000. This was an entertaining potboiler, built on Dave's experience and the theme of the consequences of not doing the unpopular and dangerous work in conservation that needed doing. He had fun with this project, but concluded he was not destined to write the Great American Novel.

Back on the serious work, he finished *RNA* and wrote a huge manuscript that he titled "Take Back Conservation" and submitted to Island Press. They rejected it. The book would be too long, it covered too wide a range of topics, and, though they likely didn't say so, the blasts of criticism leveled at the conservation movement and his sharp focus on the problem of human population growth were too hot for this somewhat staid publisher of environmental and conservation literature to handle. Dave was disappointed, disgusted, and ultimately motivated to find a way to bring to publication what he had poured into the manuscript. He would not temper his criticism, and he carved it into three books, totaling 918 pages. They were *Man Swarm and the Killing of Wildlife* (2011), *Take Back Conservation*

(2012), and *The Great Conservation Divide* (2014), all published by Raven's Eye Press.

Dave opened *Man Swarm* in his typical low-key way: "Unlooked-for but swift, we have come on like a swarm of locusts: a wide, thick, darkling cloud settling down like living snowflakes, smothering every stalk, every leaf, eating away every scrap of green down to raw, bare, wasting earth." He was similarly reserved in opening *Take Back Conservation*: "In my forty years as a conservationist, I have never beheld such a bleak and dreary lay of the land as I see today. Three whacks to my ribs bring me woe: the sinking health and wholeness of the Earth; the strength and hotheartedness of the Nature Haters; and, with the conservation band, backing down, weakness and even being taken over by the foes of wildness." In *The Great Conservation Divide*, Dave's tone was a bit more measured, but no less pointed, as he describes the history of the ideological battle in the "divide" he finds in conservation between "resourcists" and "conservationists." In the Epilogue, he opens as follows:

> So. We are done with the Public Lands Century. What comes next? Even into the second decade after the Public Lands Century, it is tough to say. I see two possibilities, both summed up in a name:
>
> The Rewilding Century
>
> The Anthropocene Century
>
> I put "Century" after each, more for the sake of consistency than by foresight. The second could end well before a hundred years have gone by, almost surely by crash. Though a crash in the History of Man is not always bad for the Tree of Life. The Rewilding Century would mean that our population growth halts and our ecological footprint lessens as we return more land and water to other Earthlings. The Anthropocene Century would mean that we wrap

> up the Human Project of fully taking over the world with little thought and no love for the millions of other kinds of Earthlings who belong here. In other words, the Great Conservation Divide carries on its struggle to the end. In the first choice (and they are indeed choices), John Muir wins; in the second the uttermost nightmare side of Gifford Pinchot wins, but in winning everything else loses.

He ends the Epilogue on a slightly more hopeful note, writing:

> So. *The Great Conservation Divide* has been a history book that ends in January 2001. My goal has been to briskly tell the tales and lay out the lessons the next generation of wildlovers needs if they are to be stronger and more winning warriors for the Wild Earth. It is a sibling to my 2004 book *Rewilding North America*, which lays out the policy and science for a hopeful, workable scientifically grounded vision for the 21st Century. Truly, more than ever before, the fate of Earth is in the hands of the generation now coming to the fore.
>
> It's up to you, my young friends and fellow Cannots. Don't let the wild things down.

Dave was passing the torch.

Soon after the publication of *The Great Conservation Divide*, a meeting was held at Dave and Nancy's home in Albuquerque to explore what might come next for The Rewilding Institute. Dave's health was not good, and if TRI was to continue, others would have to step up. At that meeting, Dave's long-time associate John Davis became the executive director of a TRI that would feature a website (rewilding.org) and tackle as many issues as it could. This was a meeting of what Dave called "Cannots," those who, as Aldo Leopold wrote long ago, cannot live without the wild. (In Leopold's

words, often quoted by Dave, "There are some who can live without wild things, and some who cannot.") The work goes on, inspired by Dave's vision. The goal, daunting as it might be, is to achieve what Dave so aptly called "The Rewilding Century."

Do We Conservationists De-wild Ourselves?

Do we conservationists end up de-wilding ourselves by softening how we portray the critters we work to protect? Do we need to ask, "Where are our teeth?" I can promise you one thing. Neither The Rewilding Institute nor I will hide our teeth. When necessary we will snarl and even bite. What this really means is that The Rewilding Institute will not hide, disguise, or prettify what we believe, what we propose, what the problems are and how bad they are, who to blame for the problems, and the essential solutions.

The Rewilding Institute is a Nature conservation organization. Period. We work to protect and restore wild species, wild habitats, and the flow and dance of evolution. No apologies.

– Dave Foreman
"Around the Campfire"
Issue 17, December 13, 2007

Campfire Lessons: Further Thoughts on Following Dave Foreman

John Davis

Dave Foreman, one of the bedrock conservation thinkers of the 20th century, often taught us, his friends and followers, through his column "Around the Campfire." This informal yet wise and authoritative series of essays ran in *Earth First! Journal*, then *Wild Earth* magazine, and finally the *Rewilding Earth* website (rewilding.org, where many are still posted). I was also fortunate to sit around the campfire, literally, with Dave Foreman & his wife Nancy Morton, and often other conservation luminaries as well, through the decades I worked closely with them. Below are some of the lessons I learned from Dave, as a writer and scholar, as a wilderness warrior, as a friend, and as a teacher.

Conservation is fundamentally about saving wild *Nature for its own sake*; it is about *serving* other species, protecting wild places and wild creatures. Conservation requires that we mature as a species and learn to practice *restraint*, to let places simply *be*. Yes, Nature provides many benefits to humankind, but the primary motivation for saving wildlands and wildlife should be for their own intrinsic value and beauty. As Dave put it at the end of his landmark book *Rewilding North America*, "Wilderness and wildlife, both as natural realities and as philosophical ideas, are fundamentally about human restraint. Remember that in Old English *wil-der-ness* means self-willed land and *wildeor* means self-willed beast. Our war on nature comes from trying to impose our will over the whole Earth...." Dave so deeply instilled this ethic in our shared work that I did not realize until I helped edit his book *The Great Conservation Divide* that many land and wildlife managers do not share this respectful and caring view.

We should, of course, side with John Muir in the famous Muir vs. Pinchot debate about preservation vs. conservation—except we should reclaim the word 'conservation,' which should be interpreted as Muir interpreted 'preservation.' What Pinchot saw as conservation is 'resourcism'—the sustainable use of natural resources for human good. Resourcism is fine for lands that we must exploit to meet vital human needs, but it is not adequate to protect Nature and should mostly be limited to private and corporate lands.

The highest standard for conservation is protected Wilderness, which means self-willed land, places we allow to govern themselves without our meddling. I was with Dave on many of his journeys to document roadless lands for his and fellow Earth First! co-founder Howie Wolke's great inventory in the book *The Big Outside*. It became painfully clear as we traveled remote public lands that roads are the beginning of the end for self-willed land. Wilderness need not be pristine—few if any places on Earth still are—but it does need to be allowed to evolve as it would naturally. Ecological restoration practices are needed in many places, sometimes even in designated Wilderness, but in Wilderness, at least, the goal should be lands and wildlife unaltered by human activities. We should practice restoration where needed, then step back and let Nature evolve freely—put Earth first!

The most urgent type of conservation work is *rewilding*, a term Dave coined in the late 1990s. Dave's shorthand definition for rewilding was *wilderness recovery*. For Dave, rewilding meant protecting and restoring huge, connected cores and swaths of wild country, replete with the full biota, including top carnivores like wolves and great cats. This, Dave insisted, we must do on land and at sea, worldwide.

In the United States and Canada, at least, and probably in much of the world, conservation reserve networks should be based on fully protected *public lands*, particularly Wilderness Areas and National Parks. A basic goal for conservationists is to expand, reconnect, and better protect public lands. By phasing out commercial exploitation of public lands, the US and Canada could meet "Nature Needs Half" goals quickly. In his chapter "The Importance of Wilderness Areas" in *Rewilding North America*, Dave carefully explains why "wilderness and national parks are the bedrock underlying protection of biodiversity and rewilding."

Conservation is a conservative, not a revolutionary, ideal. (This is a lesson from Dave with which I've struggled the most, fearing deep down that global industrial civilization is fundamentally incompatible with the natural world.) Conservation was and should again become a non-partisan issue. By late in his life, Dave had given up on the Republican Party for having become anti-science and anti-Nature, but earlier in life he was politically conservative, even having led his college's student body in electing Barry Goldwater as President.

Human overpopulation is the fundamental cause of the extinction and climate crises. Waste and over-consumption by affluent people are basic problems, yes, but we cannot stop species from sliding into extinction or climate from unraveling, a related problem, as long as we are orders of magnitude too many. Dave outlined his case for population stabilization and reduction as necessary steps toward reversing the extinction crisis in his uncomfortably blunt book, *Man Swarm: How Overpopulation is Killing the Wild World.*

Technology cannot save us, and indeed, it likely will worsen problems. With more efficient machines, we become more efficient at exploiting Nature.

Human civilization is flawed beyond reform. Conservationists' job is not to miraculously achieve a paradigm shift and convince people to live in harmony with Nature (though of course we should all try) but to save as much land and as many species as possible in big, interconnected reserve systems given the highest possible levels of protection—Wilderness Area, National Park, Forever Wild conservation easement, and the like—and trust that many of our wild neighbors will outlast us. Our civilization—based on consuming the natural world—is probably doomed, but let's spare as many of our wild neighbors as possible and hope that the human survivors of industrial collapse will learn from history and won't repeat our mistakes.

Notwithstanding the irredeemable flaws of human society, people as individuals generally do appreciate wild Nature; biophilia is real. Thus, basing our work on the intrinsic value and beauty of wild creatures and wild places is a strategic as well as an ethical course of action. We sell conservation short when we appeal to the utilitarian values of wildlife and wild places. Dave made this case at length in his book *The Great Conservation Divide*, and summarized it in his Campfire #80, "Wild Things for Their Own Sake," where he shared one of his favorite Aldo Leopold quotes: "There are those who can live without wild things, and those who cannot." Dave added: "We are the *Cannots*—women and men and children who cannot live without wild things."

Science should guide but not limit conservation efforts. We should not deny on our maps what we know from the ground to be true. GIS maps have their place, but they cannot replace the on-ground knowledge and dedication of grassroots conservation activists and naturalists and (where they still survive) indigenous peoples. If activists are making progress in getting a public land designated as Wilderness or piecing together a wildlife corridor, do not drop it just because it doesn't make the latest cut in the fancy new GIS map. (Dave was a charter member of the Society for Conservation Biology, but he always saw as much truth in old-fashioned, mylar-covered, hand-drawn conservation proposals as in any computer-generated maps.)

Funders should strengthen but not dictate conservation efforts. Most foundations and philanthropists mean well, but they seldom have the biological and geographic knowledge that activists and naturalists have, and should give *general support*, rather than earmarking their gifts for their preferred projects. The growing influence of foundations in conservation has meant more professionalism, less passion.

Grassroots, citizen activists—many of them volunteers, some modestly paid staff for small groups, some regional representatives for national groups—should lead conservation efforts. Big professional national groups have important roles to play, helping pass federal Wilderness legislation, for instance, but they should defer to the greater local and regional knowledge of the activists and naturalists on the ground. Dave often referred back to his early conservation life at The Wilderness Society, where he learned his grassroots organizing skills, and he respected most the national leaders who let regional representatives (of which he was one) lead efforts in the areas where they were the experts.

While public lands provide much—ideally, most—of the base for viable conservation reserve networks, private lands conservation is also crucial, and in some cases may afford rewilding opportunities not available on public lands. In the US East, wildways will need to be pieced together largely, sometimes mostly, from private lands. Thus, strong incentives for strong conservation of private lands are urgently needed. Wildlife-friendly farming, like that promoted by the Wild Farm Alliance, of which Dave was a senior advisor, is often needed for buffer zones, or compatible use areas, surrounding core reserves and wildways. In his work on conservation area designs in the Southwest, Dave promoted predator-friendly ranches, such as those begun by Drum Hadley and Ted Turner, as compatible with rewilding. As well, Dave was a big fan of the Northern Jaguar Reserve, comprised of former ranches and buffered by predator-friendly ranches in northern Sonora, Mexico.

All wildlands are worthy of our utmost efforts at protection, but because time is short and resources limited, we do well to focus on regional and continental wildways achievable in the near term. As Dave sketched the original "mega-linkages" (agreeing to the more poetic term 'continental wildways' after too many readers thought he was talking about large tubular meat products), they were the Spine of the Continent (Rocky Mountains and adjacent grasslands and deserts; Dave's own highest priority, and also that of his friend and rewilding conspirator Michael Soulé); Pacific Crest and Coast (Sierra and Cascades and north through coastal British Columbia and Southeast Alaska); Boreal/Arctic, across much of Canada and Alaska (and with similar opportunities in Eurasia); and Atlantic/Appalachian/Adirondack, or Eastern Wildway. Some of us were urging, and Dave was keenly interested to study, the potential for Great Plains and Gulf Coast Wildways, in what we hoped would be a second edition of Dave's landmark book *Rewilding North America* (twenty years after he wrote it, it is still the closest thing to a plan for implementing Half Earth goals on our continent). Dave also argued for vast interconnected no-take marine protected areas, or ocean wildways, now also called *swimways*.

Conservation and environmentalism are complementary but distinct movements. Environmentalism is primarily oriented toward protecting natural resources for people—highly desirable, but not altruistic. Conservation, again, is about protecting the homes and ways of other life forms. Dave's distinction here, between the conservation and environmental movement, was strategic. Dave was both a conservationist and an environmentalist, but he identified with conservation and argued we'd have more support from political conservatives (who have disproportionate influence over land and wildlife management agencies) if we treated environmentalism as a distinct movement—reflecting again his conviction that conservation should not be partisan, that it should appeal to everyone who loves wildlife and wild places, whatever their identity and political conviction.

For conservationists to ally themselves with one political party, as American conservationists (and environmentalists perhaps even more) have with the Democratic Party, is politically foolish. Republicans are basically anti-conservation these days, in part because conservationists (and environmentalists) cast our lot with Democrats. Republicans know they won't get our vote, so they do nothing for us. To me, Dave expressed this as a little more chicken and egg. He told me he thought both parties were messed up, especially in their extreme fringes.

Human justice issues are important and worthy of everyone's support, but in the US, at least, they are distinct from conservation issues. Many more groups and people are speaking out for underprivileged people than for wild species. Our job as conservationists is to speak out for wild species, however active we as individuals may want to be on important but separate social issues. This was perhaps Dave's most contentious argument, and many conservation and environmental leaders take different perspectives on this, such as Gary Nabhan and Jack Loeffler, who believe cultural diversity and biological diversity are equally deserving of efforts for protection, both serving the end of flourishing human and natural communities.

Field work is essential to conservation. We must know the places we seek to protect. We should spend at least as much time in wildlands as we do at our desks. Wilderness leave is not vacation; it is personal restoration, essential to the effectiveness of all able-bodied conservation activists. The public lands fieldwork that Dave and Howie Wolke did for their opus *The Big Outside* was monumental in scale, done in concert with local activists disclosing millions of acres of roadless lands that ought to be designated wilderness, and some of which have been since their book came out.

We should all support visionary Wilderness proposals like America's Red Rock Wilderness Act, championed by Southern Utah Wilderness Alliance, and Northern Rockies Ecosystem Protection Act, led by Alliance for the Wild Rockies, and Maine Woods National Park, advanced by RESTORE:

The North Woods; but in the main, we will need to piece together regional and continental wildways in increments. Conservationists no longer have the political clout (owing partly to our increased professionalism and our tying ourselves to the US Democratic Party) to pass sweeping national legislation, like the Wilderness Act of 1964 or the Alaska National Interest Lands Conservation Act of 1980. Wildways will be assembled by many groups using a wide range of tools, from public lands expansions and designations to conservation easements to government programs that pay landowners to retire marginal farmlands and let trees grow. Implementing a wildlands network design, Dave often said, was like assembling a jigsaw puzzle. The wildlands design was the picture on the box containing the puzzle; the puzzle itself involved numerous groups and measures—all with the generosity of spirit to dedicate ample lands and waters to the well-being of our wild neighbors.

John Davis, Executive Director, The Rewilding Institute;
Rewilding Advocate, Adirondack Council

It Was Just Like the Old Days

Jason Kahn

The weekend I first met Dave Foreman back in 1990 happened to be the weekend I had tickets to see a different legend. BB King was playing locally, and I was excited to see his show. However, a good friend called and asked what I would be doing that weekend. Going to see BB King, I answered. "I don't think so," was the reply, "you should come with me to meet Dave Foreman; he's going to be in Rowe, Massachusetts. Let's go up there instead." So, I swapped a blues legend for a conservation legend. It ended up being the right choice.

Our first oration from Dave was a fiery yet humorous, Mark Twain-like sermon in which Dave claimed to "...eat two Maxxam executives for breakfast when he was in proper health." We were all hooked. The revelations shown to us that weekend were clear, deep, and prescient. Speaking on behalf of the wolf and the redwood were among our most important responsibilities. The need to protect the land on which these species depend saves not only the wolf and redwood but all species that call the redwood forest home. When asked why we're not concerned with the people who also live in these regions, Dave answered that there are a thousand good organizations already at work protecting our fellow humans; his priority, our priority was to protect the other lives in these regions. It was as sensible as it was simple. We will work on behalf of the dusky seaside sparrow, the Kemp's ridley sea turtle, and the American chestnut tree. I felt as though I had been saved that weekend—from what I'm not sure, but I had a genuine purpose after that weekend.

Soon after Dave's inspiring visit, the Northeast had a new chapter of Earth First!. The Greater Adirondack Bioregion Earth First! was hatched, and I met two of the best friends I would ever know. Dave was involved with us as a mentor, and his interest in the Adirondacks and New England sparked during this time when he made several trips to the region. With Dave's guidance and the help of Steve Trombulak and Reed Noss, we developed the Laurentian Wildlands Reserve and map. The documents created were a series of core reserves, linkages, and buffer zones that linked and protected the wildlands from the Catskills & the Adirondacks through Vermont, New Hampshire, and into northern Maine. The plan extended across the border into Canada's Ontario, Quebec, and Labrador regions. It was a bold, beautiful image of what could be, of what should be, in anticipation of the Half Earth concept that would enlighten us further in the next decade or so.

Drawing me in deeper, I was invited by Dave and Nancy to join them on a float trip down the Green River through Desolation and Gray's Canyon. For 11 idyllic days, we rowed, paddled, and naturalized with the likes of Dave and the legendary Michael Soulé. We explored the canyon, side canyons, Fremont ruins, and abandoned ranches. We dined on some of the best food I'd ever eaten, and the daily Happy Hours were joyous. Dave and Michael would hold court at the river's edge, going back and forth between philosophizing, botanizing, and river ecology, a beer or cocktail in hand, all of us in lawn chairs or standing waist-deep in the Green, reflecting on the day's journey or tomorrow's rapids. We were genuinely bummed out when, at last, we saw the takeout and our vehicles around the next bend. Slides taken on that trip were used in my Earth Science classes for a decade or so when I was comparing and contrasting for my students the Colorado Plateau and the Allegheny Plateau. Similar geologies, yet different climates make all the difference between these two landscape regions. There isn't a week that goes by when an image of that trip doesn't make its way into my daily thoughts or dreams at night. Whenever I sleep in a tent at night when the breeze is blowing gently, I can still feel the raft responding to the wind on the Green River, how it would slowly yaw to one side or the other. To this day, almost 30 years later, I am constantly feeling the tug of the river on me while I sleep outdoors.

The last memory I have of meeting in person with Dave is from 2019, when John Davis and I were visiting Dave and Nancy in Albuquerque, a few days prior to The Rewilding Institute's annual meeting at Susan Morgan and John Miles' home in Arroyo Hondo. Dave suggested we drive south to see the Bosque Del Apache National Wildlife Refuge. It was early November, and the sandhill cranes should be there in force. A quick stop for breakfast

Captain Dave floating the Chama © Jack Humphrey

at The Owl and an hour or two later we were slowly driving the loop road at Bosque Del Apache. Snow geese and sandhill cranes were everywhere. We walked on trails and came upon a family of javelina snuffling around the forest floor for nuts. So far it was a great day. Then, shortly before sunset, when I thought we would leave, Dave said, "One more stop. I think you'll like this." We drove a few minutes to the large marsh and walked into the cane and down to the observation pier. It was there that I had the most deeply-felt wildlife experience of my life. Thousands and thousands of sandhill cranes, snow geese, and ducks of all varieties—black, mallard, merganser, shoveler, pintail—all flying in and settling in for the night on the area's largest body of water. The sound was cacophonous, each species conversing with its kind; every second a new raft of waterfowl congregated next to an even larger raft of other birds. This went on even after the sun had set. Dave led us to this spot and had the presence of mind to not talk to either of us, to let us see and hear and feel everything before us just as we should, without narration, without guidance. My eyes watered while it was happening. Seeing sandhill cranes in these prehistoric numbers had been a dream of mine since 1984. While hiking through the Hayden Valley in Yellowstone, we spied a courting pair of sandhills, the male dancing for his mate. I knew then that I had a large itch that required scratching. My eyes still get damp a bit now thinking about that day at the Bosque a few years ago, and I'm so thankful for Dave's on-the-fly decision to bring us there and how he correctly guessed this would be a big deal for us. How he didn't preface the day with expectations. He just let us be present during that majestic fly-in.

When we drove back to Albuquerque that evening, we walked into the house, and Nancy asked Dave, "How was it?" Dave answered, "It was just like in the old days." For Dave it was still a big deal. How could it have been otherwise? He was Dave Foreman, and he lived for days like these.

Jason Kahn attended SUNY Geneseo, graduating with a BS in Geology in 1984, and from SUNY New Paltz with an MS in secondary education (and an unofficial minor in rock climbing) in 1992. He's been a lifelong wildlands enthusiast, enjoying a varied array of outdoor activities. Jason taught Earth Science and Physical Science for thirty years in Chatham, New York, before retiring to Amherst, Massachusetts. He's been an environmental activist and educator for most of his adult life, focusing chiefly on the Adirondack Mountains of his home state and wildlife issues in the Northeast. Jason is the President of the Board for The Rewilding Institute.

On a Necessary Letter to the Editor of *The New York Times*

Don Waller

On September 29, 2022, a week after Dave passed and a few days after an obituary appeared in *The New York Times*, Don submitted the Letter to the Editor that appears here.

The New York Times marked a colorful era in American conservation history in its obituary of Dave Foreman (see: https://www.nytimes.com/2022/09/28/us/david-foreman-dead.html). Earth First! indeed revitalized the increasingly bureaucratic environmental movement of the 80s by injecting it with spine, energy, and theater. This deserves mention—but so do Foreman's subsequent thinking and activities. Arguably, his books and founding of the Rewilding Institute and Wildlands Network advanced conservation more than his early advocacy of monkeywrenching. After endorsing "slashing tires and downing power lines" in *Ecodefense*, Foreman repudiated violence as counterproductive in *Confessions of an Ecowarrier*. Starting in the 90s, Foreman evolved to see biology as the logical and compelling basis for conservation. His *Rewilding North America* remains a superb summary of conservation biology and how to apply it to protect wild species and landscapes. In these and a dozen other books, this complex, cantankerous, and highly knowledgeable man explores the history, philosophy, and science of conserving natural habitats. Rewilding is now a household term with efforts underway around the world. The Center for Biological Diversity in Tucson and other effective conservation organizations trace their origin to Foreman's spark and sustain his clear vision. This enduring broader legacy should also be remembered.

Professor Donald M. Waller retired as the John T. Curtis Professor of Botany and Chair of the Department of Botany and the Biological Aspects of Conservation major at the University of Wisconsin–Madison. His research focuses on threats to plant and animal diversity in the Great Lakes region's forests, including habitat fragmentation, overabundant deer, climate change, and invasive species. He co-authored *Wild Forests: Conservation Biology and Public Policy*, and he co-edited *The Vanishing Present: Shifts in Wisconsin's Lands, Waters, and Wildlife*. Professor Waller is a Fellow of the American Association for the Advancement of Science and served as an Associate Editor for *Oecologia* and *Ecology Letters*, Editor-in-Chief of *Evolution*, and President of the Society for the Study of Evolution.

Big, Wild, Connected

Lavinia Currier
February 28, 2023

A furious wind howls over you, Dave.
The weather's worse than when you left us,
seas rise, lakes and rivers shrink into beds of grit.
You disembark from your kayak
on the darkening shore; a shade
yourself, yet as always ready for action,
that grin with 'le mot juste' on your lips, "Earth First!"
When your beloved wild ones are rounded up,
corralled, beaten, shot, you bellow with them, and you shout—
you didn't want to leave your country without an Eden.

Dust devils twist bitter resins from creosote and sage
throwing them skyward, while out of a desert seep
over which the giant ponderosa leans, a vapor,
sweetened by its russet vanilla-scented bark rises—
that's you! Your radical compassion
in our riled-up west is water in the desert, and sweet balm.

For all the wrong reasons, Glen Canyon
returns to its old self. You were right
to paste a black crack on the four hundred thousand
buckets of concrete, the face of a dam
that sapped the Colorado and sinned against the sacred
upstream and down. What others called a wonder
you called terminal, and now the crack's made real
we see the light shine through, and there, transparent in its shaft,
you again! waving your bottle of spirits at us.

Quixote, wild and tender to a fault
well knew his sugar from his salt—
Come! No one gets hurt, everyone has fun!

Lavinia Currier studied poetry with Robert Fitzgerald at Harvard, and she has worked between the arts and ecosystem restoration. (With her three children, she stewards farms and wildlands, working on wildlife corridors in Virginia, reestablishing native forests on Molokai, and rewilding species in the southern San Juan Mountains of Colorado.) She directed two feature films, "Passion in the Desert" and "Oka!," and she is the director of Sacharuna Foundation, supporting Indigenous peoples' rights, endangered species, and wildlife corridors.

Wolves and Wilderness

David Parsons

I've known Dave Foreman for his last 25 post-Earth First! years. We first met at his Albuquerque home in the foothills of the Sandia Mountains on the occasion of Dave's 50th birthday. That would have been in mid-October of 1996. How I got invited to that event has vanished from my memory bank. I do remember that it was a somewhat momentous birthday, as it marked the end of whatever probationary status Dave had been on and an end to his prohibition on owning a gun. I don't know whether Dave ever owned a gun, but I never saw him with one in our many encounters.

In 1996, I was six years into my stint as the Mexican Wolf Recovery Coordinator for the U.S. Fish and Wildlife Service and in the middle of developing the reintroduction plan and all the required documentation, such as the Environmental Impact Statement. We held 24 public meetings and hearings as part of that process. Dave and his followers attended some of those meetings. His evangelical, animated, and unabashed speaking style is unforgettable, and he held back no views or opinions, publicly chastising cowboy ranchers as "wimps" for being afraid of the big bad wolf. It was always a relief to have a strong contingent of wolf proponents at the public meetings where anti-wolf interests were often well represented. Having to maintain some semblance of neutrality as the government agent in charge, I always envied those like Dave who could freely express their uncensored views.

Within a year after my formal introduction to Dave at the birthday party, he led the founding of the New Mexico Wilderness Alliance (NMWA). Dave and I are exactly one year and three days apart in age—he the elder. Knowing that I would soon retire from USFWS and knowing that I would continue to be active in nature conservation advocacy in my retirement, I sought and was granted a position on the NMWA Board of Directors. My best recollection is that I joined the NMWA Board in 1998. I served for 11 years on the Board, and Dave was also a Board member for those years and more. He was "all-in" for grand-scale wilderness preservation, and his practical and strategic advice

Dave and Dave Parsons © Merri Rudd
Two Daves at a New Mexico wolf meeting, 2014

for achieving that goal was well-earned and invaluable to his fellow Board members and beyond.

Dave was especially fond of the Gila Wilderness. He served a stint as the SW Representative for the Wilderness Society living among the right-wing, nature-hating, whack jobs in Catron County, NM. Dave was able to pull this off, because in my view, he is, at his core, a very likable guy. When I attended that birthday party in 1996, I was expecting to meet a pissed-off "radical environmentalist." Instead, I met a man who could be anyone's favorite uncle.

Through his work with the Wilderness Society, Dave was instrumental in adding a large area to the proposed northern boundary of the wilderness proposal called Aeroplane Mesa. This is a stunningly beautiful juniper/pine/gramma grass mesa perched above the Middle Fork of the Gila River Canyon. Aeroplane Mesa

(Dave was always fond of telling the story of how it was named) has become my favorite entry point for my frequent backpacks into the Gila Wilderness. I have hiked across it at least 20 times and likely more. My destination is often a place called McKenna Park—another place Dave held in extremely high regard. One reason is that it is the farthest point from a road anywhere in New Mexico. It covers a 6,000-acre bench perched about a thousand feet above the West Fork of the Gila River and sports a pristine old-growth Ponderosa pine parkland maintained by a natural ground-level fire regime similar to pre-human occupation conditions. I am especially honored to be leading an expedition to McKenna Park to honor Dave and his wife Nancy in May of 2023.

Being a friend of Dave and Nancy was my gateway to river float trips. My prior water recreation experiences had been limited to an aluminum canoe on quiet rivers and lakes, but Dave and Nancy (Nancy being the principal planner) put on big river trips on big water and often in remote places. With one major exception, my participation was limited to southwestern rivers like the Chama, San Juan, and Green. Nancy's outfitting of these trips was over the top: steaks, daily cocktail hour, and ice cream on day 5—thanks to the miracle of dry ice and monster coolers. Gear included even the proverbial "kitchen sink!" Large, heavily loaded oared rafts were necessary to haul all the gear. Dave was an expert oarsman of his raft, complete with a pirate flag.

After Dave's unfortunate back injury, it was often too painful for him to row the raft. He trained me how to row his raft and took a comfortable position at the prow like a figurehead of yore on the old sailing ships. I was as happy as a clam in the captain's chair. Dave was very patient with me and put up with my many mistakes until I became reasonably proficient as an oarsman. One of those mistakes broke the blade off an expensive oar when I whacked a cliff face. While Dave was known to be quite capable of flying into a rage when he was unhappy about something or with someone, he remained totally calm when I broke that oar, chalking it up to the learning experience.

A perk of those river trips was getting to meet Dave and Nancy's various friends and colleagues, some renowned in their fields, like ecologists Michael Soulé and John Terborgh, and mega-trekker and conservation bulldog, John Davis.

The exceptional trip I mentioned above was an epic 17- or 18-day float on an extremely remote section of the Thelon River in northern Canada near the

Arctic Circle. The reason I'm uncertain about the number of days is because the arrival of the float plane to take us back to Yellowknife was a day late. As is often the case with misfortunes, there can be a bright side. In this case, our last, unplanned, night along the river delivered a spectacular show of the northern lights.

Dave loved his martinis and fine cigars, which were part of the standard gear list for every float trip. The legendary size and number of mosquitoes in the Arctic is not a myth. This necessitated the packing of a mosquito tent for lounging and eating in camp. I have a very unusual and fortunate body chemistry that renders me immune to reactions from mosquito bites—no welt, no itch. I get little sympathy for possessing that trait. Threats were made to stake me out on the beach as a mosquito decoy. The alternative was the so-called "mosquito tent." Others already knew that a mosquito tent does not actually keep the mosquitoes out but that its dark roof and screen mesh sides cause the mosquitoes to try to escape and cling to the inside of the screen mesh. The cigars, it turned out, had an important function beyond smoke ring-blowing competitions. The cigar smoke aided in forcing the mosquitoes to the netting and keeping them there. Knowing this, Dave brought a generous supply of cigars, and we all became cigar smokers on that trip!

This float trip was special in other ways. I was allowed to bring two of my young adult sons along to experience this incredible adventure. We saw lots of wildlife, including grizzly bears, wolves, musk oxen, caribou, tracks of wolverine, and lots of birds.

I would be telling none of these stories if I had not known Dave and Nancy.

The final chapter of my special connection with Dave Foreman followed his founding of The Rewilding Institute as a landscape-scale, conservation/rewilding think-tank in 2003. I retired from the USFWS in late 1999 and wished to remain engaged in conservation work from an advocacy, non-governmental perspective. To do this, I found funding but needed to be affiliated with a registered, tax-exempt, non-governmental organization to accept the funds. I approached Dave and asked if I could be the Rewilding Institute's Carnivore Conservation Biologist if I found my own financial support. Dave instantly approved the request, and to this day I retain that title. The money has dried up, but there is no end to the necessary advocacy work.

Serendipity is often the major driver of one's life trajectory and this is certainly the case with my introduction to Dave Foreman (and Nancy). My life has been enriched in many ways by my personal and professional relationship with Dave over the last quarter century. Though Dave is gone, his good deeds on behalf of wild nature will live on forever. We should all strive for such a legacy.

My last in-person conversation with Dave was three days before he died. In that conversation, I assured him of that enduring legacy. May he rest in peace in a beautiful wild place!

David Parsons received his Bachelor of Science degree in Fisheries and Wildlife Biology from Iowa State University and his Master of Science degree in Wildlife Ecology from Oregon State University. Dave is retired from the U.S. Fish and Wildlife Service, where from 1990-1999 he led the USFWS's effort to reintroduce the endangered Mexican gray wolf to the American Southwest.

He is the Carnivore Conservation Biologist for The Rewilding Institute, a member of the Science Advisory Board of Project Coyote, a former member and chairman of the Board of Directors of the New Mexico Wilderness Alliance, and a former graduate advisor in the Environmental Studies master's degree program at Prescott College. Dave serves as a science and policy advisor for organizations and coalitions advocating for wolf recovery and landscape-scale conservation in the Southwest.

In 2001, Dave received the New Mexico Chapter of The Wildlife Society's annual "Professional Award." In 2007, at the North American Wolf Conference, Dave received the "Alpha Award" for his "outstanding professional achievement and leadership toward the recovery of Mexican wolves." In 2008, he received the "Outstanding Conservation Leadership Award" from the Wilburforce Foundation and the "Mike Seidman Memorial Award" from the Sky Island Alliance for his conservation achievements. And in 2019, Dave received the "Leader of the Pack" award from Project Coyote.

Hollywood Should Film All Westerns in Spain

A good way to get our message across might be to point out the irony that all along we have pretended that Europe was overcivilized and denatured while the American West was wild. In truth, there are 15,000 to 18,000 wolves in Europe; 2,000 wolves roam Spain alone. What sissies our wolf-hating he-men and she-women of the West really are. For authenticity, Hollywood should film all Westerns in Spain instead of in such domesticated places as Wyoming and New Mexico.

– Dave Foreman
"Around the Campfire"
Issue 12, July 4, 2007

It's in the Mail

Susan Morgan

For many years, John Davis and I have been editing Dave's manuscripts and other writing. It has been a privilege and a learning experience all along. I wish it weren't over, but perhaps we will eventually discover unfinished drafts in the archives that we've been preparing for the Dave Foreman Conservation Collection at the Denver Public Library.

In 2008, I was living in Washington State, about a half hour up the Mt. Baker Highway from Bellingham. A large package had arrived at the post office, a white reinforced envelope with tape on one edge, addressed to me in Dave's distinctive handwriting. I took it home, opened it, and unwrapped a package containing a wet suit from REI. The tags were still on it, and the size was small. I held it up, then tried it on, and sure enough, it fit.

Well, it does rain in Washington—65 inches annually at my cabin. Lots of folks have wet suits for kayaking or floating the Nooksack and Skagit. Nevertheless, it was a bit unexpected. I called my long-time friend and now husband, John Miles, in Bellingham, and told him of the present. "Hmm," John said. "That's nice. Very thoughtful."

I waited a day, gathered my thoughts, and called Dave. He wasn't home, so I left a message on his voicemail. "Thank you, Dave. This wet suit is a lovely present. You are so thoughtful, and I'll call you back!" I waited two more days and called again. He answered. "Hi, Dave, this is Susan!" After the niceties, I thanked him profusely, and what ensued was a five-minute conversation between two people who had known each other since the early 1970s and had been great friends and collaborators ever since—and who didn't have a clue what the other was saying. We were very polite, the whole time trying to figure out what we were talking about.

Then, Dave had a revelation. "Susan!" he said, "Did you ever receive my manuscript for *Take Back Conservation*?" I hadn't. He had wrapped up the thick copy and sent it as a thank-you for editing. Apparently, the USPS has offices here and there where they assemble envelopes and materials that have come apart in the mail and lay them all out on a table and try to match them up. Wet suit, Washington… So, I received a new wet suit, and some unsuspecting person opened their package to find an autographed copy of *Take Back Conservation* by the infamous Dave Foreman.

To this day, I wonder what they made of their wonderful gift.

Susan Morgan, Ph.D., studied Southwest archaeology and holds degrees in English and a Ph.D. in environmental studies. In 1967, she began her career as Director of Education for The Wilderness Society, where she worked for over ten years, and she has subsequently worked in education and outreach positions with wilderness, wildlands, and public lands conservation organizations. She is a former long-time president of The Rewilding Institute.

Bigger Than Life

Eileen Crist

Only by encouraging wilderness recovery can we learn humility and respect, can we come home at last, and can the grand dance of life continue in all its beauty, integrity, and evolutionary potential.

– Dave Foreman

I suspect that sometime as a young man Dave realized that there are two choices in life: plain life and bigger than life. He chose bigger than life and never looked back. "Bigger than life" never needs to compromise, and indeed never even contemplates that option. "Bigger than life" throws away the Washington, DC suit, the power lunches, and the mealy-mouth lobbying, heading instead for mountains, rivers, and deserts—and for direct action. No wonder Dave was part of the inspiration for a character in an Ed Abbey novel. It's the kind of thing that can happen to those who choose bigger than life.

Because he was bigger than life, Dave envisioned rewilding and coined the word. He simply *had* to see beyond the destruction—to what is possible for the planet on the other side of humanity's desolation and disrespect of the wild. His gift to us of rewilding was perhaps his greatest gift of all, being the gift of a beautiful future. What's more, his timing could not have been better. He gave the world the vision, the word, and the intent of rewilding *exactly* when it was most needed: at a time when wilderness was being disparaged both as idea and reality, by a cast of academics marshaling the fascist trope of "political correctness" to get the cowering and the unsuspecting to abandon wilderness defense. Wilderness, we were told by those foggy thinkers, separates humans from nature and was invented by white colonizers to cast out native people from their homes. Quite to the contrary, however, wilderness is the reality of wildeors and of aboriginal free geographies that urgently need protection from the rampage of *Wetico* human supremacists who have scoured the Earth and devastated First People, in tandem.

Be that as it may, echoing the physical destruction of wilderness by the dominant culture, academic deconstructionists have profoundly damaged the aspiration for freedom that underskirts wilderness reparation. That damage is still with us for the time being.

Enter rewilding: the concept and its spirit that Dave imparted, which have been spreading like wildfire. It's as if people of all ages and walks of life—having seen the idea of wilderness defiled and proscribed—were just waiting for a pristine word to run with for the exuberant and free more-than-human world restored. Of course, within the vision of rewilding beats the heart of wilderness, for rewilding is all about removing the obstacles and facilitating the ecological conditions, within landscapes and seascapes, for nature to take the reins and run the cosmic show.

I met Dave once, in 2013, at a Bioneers workshop in San Luis Obispo, California. He'd been invited to give the plenary talk. Some days prior to that evening event, he and I walked by the ocean and talked about our shared love for underwater sightseeing. Dave was a diver, and I enjoy snorkeling, if "enjoy" is the right word for snorkeling in a world whose coastal biodiversity has been bludgeoned and its vibrant colors blotted out. After trading stories of underwater glimpses of sharks, Dave said something that made me smile: "I'll swim with sharks, but I won't swim with crocs." Sensible advice that I remember often when playing in the Pacific waves of Costa Rica near where rivers flow into and mix with the sea.

What I remember most vividly from that gathering was Dave's plenary. All of us in attendance gathered outdoors, just before sunset, in an amphitheater-like setting to hear him speak. I was surprised to see Dave enjoying a cocktail just before heading for the podium; I thought it a strange thing to have a drink before giving a talk. But soon enough we all found our seats, and Dave stepped onto the stage. It was not a talk he gave—it was a sermon for the wild, flawlessly delivered.

The image that stayed with me from Dave's fiery paean was of an immense tree he once saw in Mexico. As he described it, I saw it clearly in my mind, not especially tall but of immense canopy breadth, and bejeweled with uncountable leaves, as many as the stars viewable on that cloudless night. Almost as innumerable, he reported, were the chickadees that flitted and played and chattered amongst the branches. Dave was elated by the memory of this encounter, and his audience was right there with him, mesmerized. Suddenly he started to imitate the chickadees, shaking his shoulders and vocalizing wildly. It was so moving and so funny at the same time.

I know what Dave was doing. He was conjuring an image of Earth's living abundance and vitality wrapped inside the glory of a single, bird-laden, dome-shaped vibrant tree. Abundance and vitality are what wilderness is all about. Rewilding is that reality restored.

Dave was fond of saying (quoting Aldo Leopold) that "there are some who can live without wild things, and some who cannot," and that he was decidedly in the latter camp. We might amend Leopold's statement: *No one can live without wild things.* Wild things are the source of life's creativity, regeneration, resilience, dynamism, magic, and endurance. Annihilating wilderness and wild creatures by humanizing and disenchanting the Earth severely impoverishes the manifestations of complex life and renders continued existence precarious. May humanity realize this truth soon enough instead of waiting to find out the hard way. May rewilding become a household word, and with rewilding projects multiplying, may planetary healing unfold.

Eileen Crist taught in the Department of Science, Technology, and Society at Virginia Tech for 22 years, retiring in 2020. Her work focuses on the biodiversity crisis and destruction of wild places, pathways to halt these trends, and ways forward toward creating an ecological civilization. She is co-editor of a number of books, including *Keeping the Wild* (2014) and *Protecting the Wild* (2015). She has authored and co-authored numerous academic papers as well as popular writings, is Associate Editor of the online journal *The Ecological Citizen*, and blogger for *Earth Tongues*. Her most recent book, *Abundant Earth: Toward an Ecological Civilization*, was published by the University of Chicago Press in 2019. For more information and publications, visit her website www.eileencrist.com.

Dave Shared My Love of Maps

Kurt Menke

Lovingly referred to as "Uncle Dave," Dave Foreman was an inspirational figure and mentor. I was proud to call him a colleague and friend. He was a giant in the conservation movement and famous for his fiery barn-burning speeches. At the 50th anniversary of the Wilderness Act, he opined on chickadees, whom he considered his friends. He said he was fluent in chickadee, and he brought the house down when he ended his plenary speech with a raucous "Chickadee dee dee!" call-and-response with the audience. He had a gift for creating these inspirational moments.

Dave's many accomplishments include co-founding Earth First!, The Wildlands Project, the New Mexico Wilderness Alliance, and The Rewilding Institute. He was the first to coin the now ubiquitous term "Rewilding" and authored more than 10 books including, *Ecodefense: A Field Guide to Monkeywrenching*, *Rewilding North America*, *The Big Outside*, *Confessions of an Eco-Warrior* and *Lobo Outback Funeral Home*. He wrote countless inspirational articles over decades, including his column in *Rewilding Earth*, "Around the Campfire."

Dave was the holder of the big vision, continental scale rewilding. He respected all living things, which he called "wildeors," an Old English word that he thought described them better than any modern term. He preached that "wildeors" have an inherent right to exist on their own terms and dedicated his life to making that case for wild nature. I also came to know Dave as a very kind, generous, and gentle human being. Some of my fondest memories are of sitting with a cup of coffee in his kitchen and watching the birds in his yard.

I first heard Dave speak in the late '80s at an Earth First! rally at the University of New Mexico. His message resonated deeply, and it is a memory I will always cherish. I met him in the late '90s at a New Mexico Wilderness Alliance Board Meeting while camping near the Apache Kid Wilderness in New Mexico.

Dave shared my love of maps, and soon after meeting him, I began working with him on mapping projects. His encyclopedic knowledge of the wilderness movement and of wild places on the landscape never ceased to amaze me. I learned so much about the history of conservation and protected lands from him. His back-of-the-napkin map of protected lands of the West was impressively accurate, and our discussions of maps and their importance inspired me to launch my conservation GIS consulting business, which kept me busy until I moved to Denmark in 2020. Dave would often meet me at my office, or I would go to his house in Albuquerque to gleefully pore over maps and strategize. I am incredibly proud to have produced maps for several of his books. Sadly, we were about to embark on maps for the 2nd edition of *Rewilding North America* when he passed away.

One thing that always impressed me was how his strategies evolved with the times, from Earth First! to The Wildlands Project to the Rewilding Institute. He knew when to work from the sidelines versus taking the main stage and when a new direction was required. At his core, he was an unapologetic advocate of wild beings, never caring if wolves, for instance, were politically unpopular. He was the fiercest advocate for large carnivores and top-down regulation that I have known.

In the early 2000s, we worked closely on the New Mexico Highlands Wildlands Network Vision, which is still one of my proudest achievements. Nearly 20 years later, these wildland network visions remain the boldest analyses that have been done of how to restore functional ecosystems at a landscape scale in the Southwestern US. We continued to work on Wildlands Network Visions for the Sky Islands, Southern Rockies, and Grand Canyon Ecoregion. Later, he strongly supported our local wildlife corridor work with the Tijeras Canyon Safe Passage Coalition.

Dave, thank you for being such a consistent champion for the wild. It will take me a long time to mourn your loss. You inspired my generation. I hope people hear your message for generations to come.

After running a successful GIS consulting business in the US, Kurt Menke recently moved to Denmark and now works with Septima.

He has a broad skillset as a spatial analyst, cartographer, teacher, and author. His focus has always been conservation GIS, and he has worked for most of the conservation non-profits in the Western US over the last 25 years. Kurt is an expert in modeling wildlife habitat and wildlife corridors and is an open-source GIS author, recently writing his eighth and ninth books on the software QGIS: the second editions of both *Discover QGIS 3.x* and *QGIS for Hydrological Applications*, both with Locate Press. In 2015, he became an OsGeo Charter Member.

Dave Foreman, Scholar Extraordinaire

John C. Miles

My knowledge of and relationship with Dave Foreman was different from that of many who memorialize him here. I met Dave in 1973 when budding activists like us were invited by The Wilderness Society to participate in a training workshop in Washington, DC. TWS staff, Doug Scott foremost among them, taught us the ins and outs of lobbying and about the work the Society was doing. The upshot was that many of us trainees were recruited by TWS as staff, and while Dave went to work as the Southwest Field Rep, I returned to my university faculty position at Western Washington University in Bellingham, Washington.

In that role, a decade later, I was teaching courses in environmental ethics and conservation history, and learning about deep ecology, the new field of conservation biology, and this "radical" activist organization called Earth First! that was embracing these disciplines. I knew a lot about the history of the conservation movement, and I immediately realized that this new brand of conservation activism and its philosophical underpinnings were taking the movement in important new directions. I incorporated discussion of this into my courses and learned that the fellow I had briefly met, Dave Foreman, was a leader of this whole business.

I became dean of our small college in 1985, which consumed me, but one day in 1987 I was to meet with the local Mount Baker-Snoqualmie National Forest District Ranger, and he came into my office in a rage. "What the hell are you doing sponsoring Earth First!?" he asked with considerable vehemence. He had seen a notice of an Earth First! meeting on the wall as he was entering our building. The college was not a "sponsor" of Earth First!, but there was a student organization that embraced that cause, and it was meeting in our building. I eventually calmed him down, pointing out that we could not dictate what student organizations formed or where they met on campus. He begrudgingly accepted my point, then lectured me on what a threat this "eco-terrorist" organization was to the good work of the Forest Service and other land managers. I had my own concerns about the Forest Service, which was logging the hell out of our Pacific Northwest forests at the time.

I followed what Earth First! was doing in our region as best I could and shared what I was learning with the students. The essence of that was that this band of activists was, in its thinking and its actions, changing the aims of conservation, from protecting nature for its human values, such as recreation and useful resources, to protecting biological diversity and intrinsic values. As a member of the board of the National Parks and Conservation Association in the late '80s and early '90s, I could see what a large, relatively conservative national organization could accomplish—which was important and almost entirely anthropocentric—but also what was needed beyond working toward conventional conservation goals using conventional methods.

When Dave left Earth First! and the journal *Wild Earth* was launched in 1991, I began to really follow, understand, and appreciate what he and his *compadres* were doing. I especially enjoyed his "Around the Campfire" with its wide-ranging style. In the first issue of *Wild Earth*, Dave wrote that "During the last decade new conservation groups have sprung up like owl clover in the desert after a wet winter." He named some of the groups, then noted that they "are working in a variety of ways for the preservation of natural diversity and the careful design of preserves to protect that diversity. Scenery and primitive recreation are incidental to their agenda." This he called the "New Conservation."

Reading *Wild Earth*, and following the emergence of The Wildlands Network, confirmed for me that something big was happening—a new approach to conservation grounded in conservation biology. I was struck, in reading Dave's writings, with the breadth of his knowledge and the creativity of his thinking. I came to see him as an independent scholar, deeply curious, a great synthesizer of ideas, and a writer. (I had not, until 2008, heard him speak, clearly another of his gifts.) Dave's scholarship was not driven by any motivation except a deep-seated desire to protect the natural world and wilderness, basing rationales for that protection on the latest understanding of the natural world, and building strong arguments for the protection of biodiversity and methods to do so. He was not a scientist but understood the science behind the New Conservation and was comfortable surrounding himself with scientific leaders like Michael Soulé and Reed Noss, among others. His scholarship was always in service to the goals of New Conservation. He became, for me and many others, the spokesman for this movement.

Dave was a gifted and prolific writer. His style was forthright, provocative, sometimes serious, sometimes witty. He wrote (and said) what he thought needed saying, sharing what he saw as hard truths, never shying from what might be or would become controversial. He could really turn a phrase, and his research was impressive. The work, much of it on the ground, that he and Howie Wolke did for *The Big Outside* was remarkable—nobody had done anything like it since Bob Marshall in the 1930s. The scope of *Rewilding North America* was extraordinary, and the book was full of groundbreaking ideas, some of which have seen fruition (though as Dave struggled to come out with a new edition in his last years, he lamented that he had not made more progress).

Dave loved language, especially Old English. He kept a well-thumbed Old English dictionary on the table next to his chair. His penchant for such language sometimes frustrated the editors, of his last three books, Christianne Hinks, John Davis, and Susan Morgan, who thought some of this language would confuse readers. They usually prevailed.

Dave had so much to say that the manuscript for a book he titled "Take Back Conservation" grew to such size that his publisher of *Rewilding North America* rejected it as too big and far-ranging. Undaunted, Dave reworked the material into three books, *Manswarm and the Killing of Wildlife* (2011), *Take Back Conservation* (2012), and *The Great Conservation Divide* (2014). These were published by The Rewilding Institute and Ravens Eye Press.

Another most impressive Foreman quality was his encyclopedic memory. I served on The Rewilding Institute Board for four years, and we convened almost weekly Zoom "worker bee" meetings to discuss issues and strategy.

Dave joined many of these meetings in the role of elder statesman and font of information about myriad topics. Someone would ask him a question, and he would lean back in his chair and be off, sharing a wealth of knowledge about wild America (gathered long ago for *The Big Outside*), relevant insights from conservation biology, or detailed knowledge of wildlife, with nary reference to a note.

My admiration for Dave as a scholar was confirmed and grew after Dave passed away when Christianne Hinks, Susan Morgan, and I took on the task of pulling together his "papers" for deposit in the Dave Foreman Collection of the Conservation Collection in the Denver Public Library. Dave's papers were not very well organized—I got the impression that he had so much to do that he didn't want to spend any more time than necessary organizing his stuff. But the many drafts of his manuscripts and the scale of the research resources he had gathered, as well as his extensive library with books festooned with Post-it notes, were most impressive. Some of his material is already archived at the University of New Mexico and the Denver Public Library, and before long the DPL collection will be extensive and invaluable to researchers.

I consider Dave a "scholar extraordinaire" because he exemplifies the activist scholar who does not pursue research primarily to expand human knowledge, which is a good thing of course, or to "publish or perish" as in the academic sphere, but purely in pursuit of a righteous cause. Dave didn't get rich—thankfully he had Nancy, herself a powerhouse, who supported him in so many ways over the years—and he did win a measure of fame, mostly in what some considered the "infamy" of his Earth First! days. But he wasn't especially interested in fame or fortune. He sought to advance the cause, and he certainly did.

As a lifelong member of the academic world, I have only the greatest admiration for what Dave accomplished in the many dimensions of his work. I want to say "career," but that wouldn't be right. Echoing Jack Loeffler, Dave "didn't have a career, he had a life." Back in my university administrator days, knowing what I know of him today, I would certainly have wished he were part of our faculty. But he wouldn't have wanted that. It would be too confining—he would not have been publishing in the proper journals. I probably couldn't have hired him because he lacked proper academic credentials, foolish as that would have seemed to me.

Dave found his way as a wildeor, exactly as he should.

John C. Miles taught for over four decades at Huxley College of the Environment (now titled The College of the Environment at Western Washington University), for over four decades. He has worked on conservation issues, mostly in the Pacific Northwest, since the late 1960s, especially park and wilderness issues in the North Cascades. Author and/or editor of seven books, he has served on the boards of many environmental education and conservation organizations, the NPCA, The Rewilding Institute, and North Cascades Institute among them, and for a decade he was the General Public Member of the Washington Forest Practices Board which is charged with regulating the private timber industry in that state. In retirement, he lives near Taos in northern New Mexico with his wife and colleague, Susan Morgan.

The New Mexico Wilderness Alliance

In 1995, Dave Foreman and Susan Morgan organized and hosted the first New Mexico State Wilderness Conference that Dave had been involved in since his years as Southwest Field Rep with The Wilderness Society. Many of the same issues Dave had been working on back in the 1970s were still on the docket, some of which involved the Gila Wilderness. They invited representatives from a broad array of environmental organizations and old conservation friends and acquaintances he had worked with for years.

The conference was well attended. It was divided into two parts; issues presented in the first half included the Mexican Wolf, BLM Wilderness and public lands, logging without laws, Endangered Species, and grazing; the second half explored strategies for dealing with each. Dave was a principal speaker, as were Rod Mondt and Jim Strittholt from The Wildlands Project, and Jim Baca, Lawson LeGate, and Brant Calkin, all conservation luminaries. Wendy Brown discussed the U.S. Fish and Wildlife Service program for reintroduction of the Mexican Gray Wolf, which involved local hearings to gain public support. This was a high-profile, contentious issue, and at the close of the conference, organizers rallied participants to generate support for wolf reintroduction. Dave appealed to wildlife supporters in all organizations to join the campaign against vociferous and well-organized opposition from the ranching community.

Dave's wife, Nancy Morton became central to the campaign, and Dave arranged for buses to transport supporters to a hearing in Roswell. This organizing paid off. Hearings in New Mexico, Arizona, and Texas were dominated by wolf reintroduction supporters, and eventually, reintroduction was approved.

In the two years following the wolf reintroduction campaign, Dave and Nancy lamented that little was happening in wilderness advocacy and began gathering with friends and colleagues at their home to explore and brainstorm what needed to be done to get things moving again on this front. Among those attending these early gatherings were a couple of Wilderness Study Committee board members who still serve on the New Mexico Wild board today. The first order of business for this collection of interested folks was to decide how they would organize themselves. They hatched a plan.

The group would form a non-profit outfit, hire a paid staff member, and approach the existing Wilderness Study Committee/ Wilderness Committee to propose they join the effort. The proposal passed, and Bob Howard was chosen to lead. Board members of the Wilderness Study Committee, and the former executive director, were invited to become NMWA board members. Dave, it should be recalled, had begun his conservation career three decades earlier coordinating the Wilderness Study Committee's work to expand the Gila Wilderness.

A few weeks later, everyone gathered at Dave and Nancy's home to select board members and officers and make assignments. Bob Howard was elected board chair, Jeff Regenold vice-chair, Nancy Morton secretary, and Rick Aster was named treasurer. Kathy Love and Nancy Morton agreed to draft the bylaws and submit the application for incorporation. Bob, with the help of his wife Phillenore Howard, would initially perform many of the duties of staff, handling the daily routine, managing the money, and preparing the IRS 501(c)(3) application for nonprofit status.

Dave approached Doug Tompkins and Yvon Chouinard for financial assistance. On March 23, 2000, the certificate of incorporation was approved. Ed Sullivan was hired as program coordinator in 1999 and was very effective, and Michael Scialdone (who was called "Scial") came to work as Wilderness Inventory Coordinator. Both initially lived with Dave and Nancy. In October of the same year, Tisha Broska was hired as a contractor and a "do whatever needs to be done" staff member and continues to do much the same today, 23 years later, having served for a time as acting executive director and now serving as deputy to Mark Allison, executive director.

The New Mexico Wilderness Alliance (NMWA) was officially launched, but Scial needed help. Greg Magee, a biologist and native plant specialist, left the board to become a staff member assisting with wilderness inventory. Scial divided the state into northern and southern halves, with Magee, a Las Cruces resident, assigned the south and Scial taking the north. The two trained a cadre of volunteers they recruited and completed their job in 2002, having filled two file cabinets with their reports, maps, and findings. Dave, needless to say, with his decades of experience and encyclopedic knowledge of wild New Mexico, pitched in as he could. The voluminous archive they produced was summarized in a digital document, and then it was distributed internally to federal agencies and any interested parties. This inventory has been useful ever since as the starting point for wilderness campaigns that have followed, including re-inventories of the Gila region and area surrounding the Pecos Wilderness.

Wilderness designations promoted by NMWA and its allies began slowly and the first was Sabino Wilderness, established in 2009. Then came two great National Monuments organized by NMWA with crucial support of Representative Martin Heinrich and Senator Tom Udall. These were the Rio Grande del Norte National Monument in 2013 and Organ Mountains-Desert Peaks National Monument in 2014. A bill for the Columbine-Hondo Wilderness in the Carson National Forest was introduced in 2012, with NMWA support and urging, by Senator Jeff Bingaman. This passed Congress in 2014 also with strong support from Representative

Martin Heinrich and Senator Tom Udall. Tom half-jokingly told a celebratory crowd after the legislation was approved that he saw what was moving in Congress and attached the wilderness bill to the National Defense Appropriations Act. Whatever works! A subsequent bill for Wilderness in the Rio Grande del Norte NM was also approved, and another is slowly progressing in 2023. All of these were accomplished with local help to win adjacent community support for the wilderness areas, without which passage would not have been possible. Collaboration has been an effective tool used by NMWA.

NMWA achieved truly national prominence in 2014 when it hosted the 50th Anniversary of The Wilderness Act in Albuquerque. NMWA staff spoke eloquently and introduced other presenters. The star of the show was Dave Foreman, who gave one of his stemwinding speeches at the close of the celebration. He had the crowd on its feet, moving them to cheers and tears and new resolve to continue the great wilderness work done over the past fifty years. He had been in on the action in various ways for a big portion of those years, and everyone's respect for him was clear.

Today the New Mexico Wilderness Alliance, now NM Wild, after its hardscrabble beginning, is recognized as one of the premier state wilderness groups in the country. This made Dave very proud. He was also proud of the fact that NMWA has recruited staff who live in NEW MEXICO who know and care for the communities in which they work. By developing grassroots support in various campaigns, NMWA has naturally acquired multicultural staff representative of the state. Nancy served as secretary of the board from the beginning until the last two years of her life when she was chairperson. Dave worked for a while as staff and wrote articles for the NMWA newsletter; he said it was like coming home.

A Towering Presence

Mark Allison

It is of course impossible to do much credit to anyone's life in just a few words, and particularly so for one as full and rich as Dave's.

As anyone reading this book already knows, Dave was a towering figure in the wilderness and conservation movement, with many notable contributions and achievements throughout his life. He was not just a rabble-rouser—though that in itself was significant—but a serious intellect with a deep and sustained passion and discipline spanning decades. He authored numerous works of consequence and helped to create a range of influential conservation organizations. I trust others who are more qualified will highlight the historic importance of his role, so I will instead share some thoughts about Dave as a person.

Looking to join the New Mexico Wilderness Alliance (New Mexico Wild) ten years ago, I initially found the thought of being interviewed by Dave and serving under him as a director on the board to be an intimidating one. Somewhat star-struck, I had read his books and was aware of his reputation. How, I wondered, could I as a newcomer possibly withstand his scrutiny and measure up against the fierce standards of this giant in the movement? I may have even had some notion of being castigated by a displeased fanatic, likely in his booming voice, possibly with his arms waving.

Instead, Dave was warm and welcoming to me beyond anything I had a right to expect or deserve. He was gracious and always willing to share his time. He was patient with my questions and my newness to "professional" conservation. I saw him extend this same kindness of spirit to countless others over the years.

Of course, over time, I learned he needed little prompting to regale those in earshot with stories, which more than occasionally started off "back in the 1970s…." I loved hearing all of them, recognizing even then how lucky we were to have this opportunity.

I was fortunate to spend time with Dave and Nancy on river trips and can personally confirm numerous examples of his well-deserved reputation for

Dave and Mark Allison © NMWild Staff

bumbling accident-proneness. On one occasion on the San Juan River, Dave had already contrived to injure his hand early in the trip, which Nancy had expertly taped (from what most would describe as an excessively large first aid kit, but through much experience had been determined to be just the right size with Dave along). Dave was trying to get the grill going at camp when the happy hour chatter was interrupted by Dave loudly crying out, "#&%#—my bandage is on fire!"

After expressing the requisite initial concern, the absurdity of it made it impossible to stifle laughs. And after a cold botanical gin, which Dave called a "martini," despite zero vermouth, he too found the humor in it. I liked that he was able to laugh at himself with his eyes crinkling and that hearty guffaw. And how he managed to become so filthy half an hour into a week-long trip was always a mystery to me. Paddle forward…or something!

Danger lurked closer to home too. Like the time he was trying to cat-proof his backyard and fell off the roof—not once, but twice! His long-time friends could spend days recounting stories like these, something I know Dave would welcome and take great pleasure from. He really did have nine lives. He used to say that he "wasn't old, just beat up." And it's true, he could be hard on himself.

Even before he became a published author, a significant part of Dave's advocacy was motivating others to action through speeches. Public speaking was important to Dave, and early on he resolved that he wanted to do it well. It was something he worked at very intentionally. As anyone who had the chance to hear him speak knows, he succeeded. (Speaking with Kenneth Brower after an event in Silver City some years back, Kenneth noted that the one person his father David Brower, the first executive director of the Sierra Club, did *not* want to follow as a speaker was Dave.)

Dave was a truly gifted orator, and his speeches could move people to tears and get them on their feet. He had a rare ability to resonate intergenerationally, and new and younger cohorts would lean forward in their chairs, eagerly listening to what he was saying. Reaching and exciting new advocates and stewards is one of his important legacies. After a speech, people, young and old, would clamor to connect with him. Whatever the topic, he invariably exhorted the audience to value the natural world for its own sake, apart from any human-centric lens or benefit. *Chickadee Dee Dee!*

I was able to spend time with Dave in his last days. He was dying; he knew it and told us so, and he said that he was not afraid. To the last, he was gracious and wanted us to know how proud he was of his role in helping establish New Mexico Wild and of what it had become. He expressed regret at not being able to organize his papers to completion, though to be fair, that would have taken several lifetimes. He wasn't a hoarder exactly… but let's say he was conscientious about saving. And a lifetime of work advocating for wild places and wild creatures ("wildeor") adds up, in more ways than one.

After Dave's passing, I received messages from his friends and colleagues (and from some who didn't even know him personally), several of whom used the term "North Star" to describe what Dave meant to them and to conservation in general. I think that's right. Dave shined brightly and never wavered. He didn't lose focus on what was important, and his clarity and constancy guided many of us. And, I know, will continue to do so.

Dave was not without his faults, none of us are. But he was a powerful force, a significant figure in the evolution of the conservation movement, and a contributor and proponent of big ideas, years and even decades ahead of his time—formative concepts like rewilding, biodiversity, connectivity, and of course, the essentialness of wildness. For its own sake.

Dave was a friend and a mentor to me and countless others. I will remember him for his intellect, his encyclopedic memory, his epic stories, his willingness to poke fun at himself, his easy laugh, his generosity to me and my family, and his big heart.

His passion for wilderness and his true joy and wonder at experiencing even the humblest of creatures were an inspiration to me. His lifelong commitment to advocating for their protection is the model and standard that we at New Mexico Wild and all who loved him will look to as our obligation to truly honor his memory.

Alas, though Dave wasn't able to meet his end by being trampled by a muskox on the Arctic tundra as he fairly longed for, he was able to escape the hospital to be with friends and family at home.

In some of his last words to me, he said he didn't want to be forgotten. I told him he wasn't exactly the forgettable type. I still don't know if gin without vermouth is really a martini, but here's to you, Dave. Well done.

Mark Allison is the Executive Director of New Mexico Wild, which Dave helped establish and which celebrated its 25th anniversary in 2022. He has over thirty years of professional experience working with social-profit nongovernmental organizations in leadership positions, including over twenty-three years as executive director. Before joining New Mexico Wild, Mark's activities focused on anti-poverty and social justice work, with an emphasis on developing permanent affordable housing for persons experiencing homelessness. Mark's projects earned national recognition for modeling award-winning sustainable "green" design.

Since coming to New Mexico Wild in 2013, Mark has been proud to lead a team that has helped secure numerous new protections for New Mexico's land, waters, and wildlife. Mark earned bachelor's and master's degrees in political science from Illinois State University, fell in love with New Mexico in 1977, and moved here permanently in 1993. He resides in Albuquerque with his wife, Jenny Metzler, and his two sons, Levin and Jack. He believes passionately that we have a responsibility to permanently protect land, not only for future generations to experience and enjoy but for its own sake.

Dave Foreman: Wise Guy

Bron Taylor

In two ways, Dave Foreman was a wise guy.

Adversaries and devotees alike knew him as charismatic gang leader of a criminal conspiracy.

The same was said of Mahatma Gandhi and Martin Luther King Jr., but today, their lawbreaking is widely considered to have been morally justifiable and socially salutary. So will much of the lawbreaking by environmentalists trying to prevent the collapse of Earth's living systems.

Foreman was as wise in another sense. He was a student of history, politics, ecology, and environmentalism, which led him to think deeply, strategically, and provocatively, but also in nuanced ways, about our place in the world and our responsibilities to it.

For me, he has been an exceptionally important muse. So has the movement he inspired.

Something struck a chord in me when, about 1987, I first noticed Earth First! law-breaking its way into the news. I soon found and began devouring, *Earth First!*, the movement's tabloid, which Foreman edited.

At the time, I was in graduate school focusing on anti-authoritarian, social-justice movements around the world. I had become frustrated that these movements typically ignored the exploitation of the natural world. The dearth of such concern was also evident among academicians.

I did not yet have a language to describe my own moral intuition: that the entire world has value apart from its usefulness to our own species. As when Foreman and the founders of Earth First! discovered, in the notion of 'deep ecology,' a linguistic expression for their own moral intuitions, I also immediately 'grocked' with such moral sentiments, whether they were called deep ecology, biocentrism, or ecocentrism.

My own affinity for such moral sentiments was not, however, the only reason I became interested in radical environmentalism.

I knew that social movements inspired by religion, including those that deploy disruptive and illegal tactics, sometimes precipitate dramatic, positive, social transformations—and reading the journal—I could see that there was something deeply spiritual animating many movement activists. Moreover, I thought, if the movement's projected 'rednecks for wilderness' image was accurate and mobilizing rural, working-class individuals, this could be a game changer, dramatically empowering America's environmental movement. I considered such a possibility intriguing and hopeful.

But as I learned more, I was unsure how I felt about perspectives advanced by movement intellectuals and activists.

I knew there were serious environmental problems, but were they exaggerating when they claimed humankind was precipitating massive species extinctions and even the collapse of industrial civilizations? Was the American political system so entangled with voracious capitalism that it was unable to respond to this crisis? Was this system entirely illegitimate, and therefore, revolutionary responses were necessary? Were anarchistic and bioregional social philosophies the only way forward? Were illegal strategies beyond civil disobedience, such as equipment sabotage, tree-spiking, arson, and even lethal violence, morally permissible and potentially effective? Did conservation biology provide scientific guidance for creating and connecting wildlands and lives and thus preventing further erosion of Earth's genetic and species variety?

Foreman and other movement architects also looked backward to understand how we arrived at this crisis point, proffering theories about the roots of the devastation. Were their ideas compelling? Did the destructive turn begin with the domestication of non-human organisms and the advent of agriculture and the concomitant explosion of human numbers? Did this lead humans to exceed the carrying capacities of the habitats they previously depended upon, which then led to expansionist and imperial agricultural civilizations forcibly assimilating, exterminating, or otherwise driving small-scale foraging societies from their homelands? Were anthropocentric, monotheistic, otherworldly, patriarchal, pro-natalist religions, and Western philosophies and sciences, deeply complicit in these processes? Did animistic, indigenous traditions, religions originating in Asia, or revitalized or newly invented

Paganisms, provide worldview alternatives compatible with the flourishing of life on Earth?

During the 1980s, these unsettling claims were often advanced and debated within the movement. As I was confronted by them, I was skeptical.

Then, as fate would have it, in April 1990, only a few months after I assumed an academic position at the University of Wisconsin Oshkosh, I learned that Dave Foreman was scheduled to give a talk on campus. This was, of course, only about a year after his 1989 arrest for, the FBI and Department of Justice alleged, supporting monkeywrenching in the Southwestern U.S.

I was keen to discuss the sorts of claims I had encountered in *Earth First!*, so I arranged to interview him and, since I seemed to know more about the movement than others on campus, was asked to introduce him before his public talk. During it, I saw first-hand his ability to rile up a crowd as well as how bright and thoughtful he was.

During the interview on that occasion, and in a longer one at his home in New Mexico in 1993, he was much like a professor mentoring a graduate student. (Indeed, in his areas of expertise, I was a relative neophyte.) He pointed me to a number of writers who had been formative for him.

I already knew about Aldo Leopold, having been introduced to him during the 'ethics' segment of interpretive training that all California State Park Rangers and Lifeguards went through. Foreman also mentioned Louis Mumford (on the destructiveness of technological systems), William Catton (on how humans keep exceeding the carrying capacity of their habitats, causing ecosystem collapses or forcing migrations), and Stanley Diamond and Paul Shepard (whose overlapping arguments asserted that foraging societies and their animistic spiritualities were superior to the imperial agricultures that have destroyed or displaced most such small-scale societies).

Foreman also gave me a primer on the history of wilderness conservation; the revolving-door of corruption between resource managers, extractive industry plutocrats, and politicians; and how he saw the failures of the conservation movement (too careerist and compromise-prone to stand up to 'wise-use' fanatics). He fleshed out what he thought was needed for what his compadre Howie Wolke called a 'thoughtful radicalism,' namely, one that would not be so counter-cultural as to immediately alienate regular folk.

One that would be conservation-biology informed, focused on connecting biological reserves in networks that could maintain the continents' genetic, species, and ecosystem variety. We also discussed restoration ecology and the hopeful prospect of rewilding the world.

When one considers from where in the cultural landscape of America Foreman emerged, the kind of ideas he contemplated and advanced were more than a little surprising.

The sociology of knowledge powerfully explains the power of socialization, why (to speak metaphorically) an individual human apple rarely falls far from their social tree. Such sociology also describes the processes by which some individuals manage to break out from the worldviews they inherit from those who initially socialize them.

Despite its explanatory power, however, such sociological analysis does not adequately explain why one similarly situated individual follows the herd, while only a few become contrarians. Foreman wondered that too, I think, speculating about whether there was a 'wilderness gene,' a nature-gifted affinity for wild places and wildlife that some people have that others do not.

Do some have a stronger innate biophilia, as biologist E.O. Wilson put it, than others? Or is a contrarian nature rooted more in one's experiences in the world? Many radical environmentalists, I know, describe difficult childhoods and how, in various ways, this has led them to seek companionship and healing beyond human communities. I can relate, and I've wondered whether that played a role in Foreman's own contrary nature.

Whatever accounts for a contrarian tendency, I know that I also have one. I am disinclined to adopt any perspective without subjecting it to careful scrutiny, whether it is mainstream or countercultural. My default skepticism applied, as well, to the perspectives advanced by Foreman and the eclectic, and sometimes contentious and troubled activists, who were drawn to the radical environmental movement. And although I had been moved by the civil rights and various liberation movements around the world and believed there was a time and place for civil disobedience designed to arouse the conscience of wider publics, I was a California State Park Lifeguard/Peace Officer before I became an academic, not a hippy or anarchist. I was not about to easily accept claims that environmental degradation was so grave, and the American political system so corrupt or inept, that tactics beyond civil disobedience were morally permissible, let alone effective. Indeed, I saw the law and its enforcers as a necessary bulwark against violence and environmental harm, both in and beyond Park boundaries.

In more than three decades since I first met Foreman and began my explorations of the diverse subcultures of radical environmentalism, therefore, I have sought to tease out where I agree and where I depart from the various perspectives I found within the movement. Far more often than not, I have come to agree with Foreman. Where I demur, I understand there is a reasonable basis for the other point of view, and sometimes, I wonder, whether my understanding of Foreman's understanding might be outdated.

People who think critically and recognize complexity, as Foreman clearly did, often revise their views over time based on new information. Indeed, the historian in me thinks it is important to assess how the minds of major figures have changed or remained the same over time. This is one of the reasons I was very sad when, in September 2022, I learned of Foreman's passing. I was planning to visit him again in the spring of 2023 and ask him how his mind had changed or remained the same over time. Now, I will have to ask his closest confidants how they think he would have answered such a query.

For my part, I have long felt a deep connection to nature, that all species are kin and deserve respect, and so, I deeply resonated with Foreman when he told me in 1990, "I agree with Aldo Leopold about virtually everything. A thing is right when it tends to advance the beauty, stability, and integrity of the natural community," and we should "protect the earth because we love it," noting that this was what Leopold was expressing when he wrote, "there are those who can live without wild things and sunsets and there are those who cannot." After quoting Leopold, Foreman added, "I think that's fundamentally the key. When you really love wild things, you recognize that your own life does not have meaning apart from those things."

Foreman also recognized that for our species, the love of nature is typically connected to one's spirituality. During the 1980s he expressed clear affinity with Paganism. In 1987, writing under his pen name, Chim Blea, he wrote that after rejecting Christianity he:

> flirted briefly with eastern religions before rejecting them for their anti Earthly metaphysic. Through my twenties and early thirties, I was an atheist—until I sensed something out there. Out there in the wilderness… So, I became a pagan, a pantheist, a witch, if you will. I offered prayers to the moon, performed secret rituals in the wildwood, did spells. I placated the spirits of that which I ate or used (remember, your firewood is alive, too.)… For almost ten years, I've followed my individualistic shamanism (no, organized paganism smacks a little too much of a Tolkien discussion group, or of a rudimentary "great religion" for one like me who never quite fits in). (Chim Blea, "Spirituality," *Earth First!*, 1987, v. 7, #7, p. 23)

Despite his ambivalence toward organized religion and even toward pagan ritualizing, Foreman concluded, "Nonetheless, we do seem to have a spiritual sense. Perhaps our fatal flaw, that which sunders us from Earth, is our ability for abstract thinking. To think of things as *things*. And spirituality, ritual, is that which attempts, albeit imperfectly, to reconnect us. Maybe I'll talk to the moon tonight." A year later, writing under his own name, he praised Starhawk's 1979 book, *The Spiral Dance*, which influentially promoted Wicca, and reverence for nature, in America and beyond, writing, "this isn't some weird eco-la-la tract, it's the best religious book since the burning times" (Dave Foreman, "Review of The Spiral Dance," *Earth First!*, 1988, v. 9, #1, p. 35). Foreman also had learned from and respected indigenous societies (while studiously avoiding universalizing and romanticizing indigenous people into noble savage caricatures), and he often argued that we need to "resacralize" our perceptions of the Earth.

When I interviewed him in 1993, I asked him about his experiences and the intellectuals and activists he variously drew on for his affinity with Paganism, which was evident via his insistence that the journal publish according to a (Celtic) Pagan calendar. He responded that he had become a little embarrassed by some of that enthusiasm. Perhaps he was already ambivalent about this, and this accounts for why he wrote his most personal reflections about his own pagan ritualizing under his pseudonym. I continued by mentioning how he often spoke of the Earth as sacred, and asked him what he meant by that. He answered,

> It's very difficult in our society to discuss the notion of sacred apart from the supernatural, I think that's something that we need to work on, a non-supernatural concept of sacred; a non-theistic basis of sacred. When I say I'm a non-theistic pantheist it's a recognition that what's really important is the flow of life, the process of life… [So] the idea is not to protect ecosystems frozen in time… but [rather] the grand process… of evolution… We're just blips in this vast energy field… just temporary manifestations of this life force, which is blind and non-teleological. And so I guess what is sacred is what's in harmony with that flow. (23 February 1993 interview, Tucson, Arizona)

This revealing statement shows that Foreman's spirituality evolved in an entirely naturalistic way. These words reminded me of Edward Abbey's own naturalistic pantheism. As is the case for scores of people around the world today who have left behind the metaphysical truth-claims of the world's predominant religions, myself included, Foreman expressed a spirituality of belonging and connection to nature, which provides meaning and environmentalist purpose.

Foreman also thought about sacrality in another way, recognizing that for many Americans, the American flag was sacred, or at least it reflects a sense that there was something exceptional about "the republic to which it stands." And although he was a harsh critic of American politics, and he was a person who had, like Abbey, confessed to anarchist sensibilities (writing in the masthead of *Earth First!*, for example, that the movement "does not accept the authority of the hierarchical state"), he was angry at the burning of the stars and stripes at the 1987 EF! Rendezvous. As he told me later, he recognized the power of that symbol and that the right wing, wise use movement, which wraps itself in it, ought not to be able to claim it. Foreman understood, I think, that the flag need not represent virulent religious nationalism but instead, and at its best, can represent the kind of *we feeling* and *place feeling* that can provide an affective basis for peaceful coexistence between all members of the land community.

When Foreman noted in the previously quoted passage that he "never really fit in" with the more "woo woo" factions of the movement, the same thing was true with regard to those from the anarchist or socialist left, as well as from the libertarian right. He was a radical in many ways, but this was a kind of moderate radicalism, if that notion is not too oxymoronic: Foreman's views were moderated by recognition of ambiguity and complexity, and even, I think, by intellectual humility. Ecosystems are more complex than we will ever know and so are the social systems that evolve from them, and the path to making them healthy and resilient is never as clear as a given slogan or ideology might suggest. Moreover, Foreman recognized, as do so many other conservationists, even those who have had their anarchistic phases and sentiments, that whatever tactics might lead to the protection of an ecosystem, or the rewilding of it, it will take scientific expertise, good laws, enforcement mechanisms, as well as authentic democratic political space and citizen vigilance, to protect movement victories and secure future ones.

This does not mean that Foreman outgrew his conviction that extra-legal tactics have been and can be morally permissible and effective.

It is, in my view, incontrovertible, that he and the best of the movement he inspired, through civil disobedience, tree spiking, and creative, sacrality-evoking neologisms, put the desecration of America's ancient forests into public ferment in a way they would not have been otherwise.

It is inconceivable that in the absence of this movement that there would be an Option 9 (which protected at least some old-growth forest in the Pacific Northwest), or a Roadless Rule (which Bill Clinton established due largely due to radical environmental resistance to deforestation in wilderness areas; Trump overturned it, but under the current Biden Administration it has been restored). Although inadequate, they give a number of species a fighting chance of long-term survival, including the Northern Spotted Owl.

The more scientifically inclined branch of the movement that Foreman led also played a unique and salutary role in bringing the very notion of biodiversity and its importance out of scientific journals and into public awareness and debate. This was also the case for restoration ecology, which began to get off the ground in the mid-1980s, and Foreman cleverly dubbed 'rewilding' in the early 1990s. That brilliant memorable trope has helped to catapult the idea into a global movement, which is deeply informed by the discipline of conservation biology. Foreman likewise championed the importance of such sciences during the 1980s while still editing *Earth First!*, continuing this focus during the 1990s with the Wildlands Project and *Wild Earth*, and in more recent years via the Rewilding Institute.

It is a remarkable legacy to all those who developed such models, including Michael Soulé and Reed Noss, as well as Foreman, Howie Wolke, and others who popularized such approaches, that all over America and beyond, conservationists are working to create, restore, and connect critical habitats needed for a host of endangered species.

Without Foreman and those he learned from and inspired, none of these salutary trends would be nearly as far along as they are today. In an age characterized by a 'great acceleration' of negative anthropogenic environmental change, which can be both depressing and disempowering, it is important to recognize that for many, ideas and practices once considered radical, if not also fanciful, now seem obvious and necessary. These ideas and practices may even be on the way to becoming mainstream views within the global environmental milieu.

When I first met him during his visit to Wisconsin, Foreman mentioned that there were many ways to contribute to the movement to protect life on earth, including via 'paper monkeywrenching,' such as filing lawsuits and by writing in ways that educate publics about the ecological crisis, including its philosophical and religious roots, and salutary alternatives. Before he left town, I handed him a copy of his book, *Ecodefense*, and asked if he would sign it. In it, he scrawled, "Keep wrenching those young minds." I've done my best.

Indeed, in these efforts, Dave Foreman, and the intellectuals and activists he variously drew on and inspired, and to whom he introduced me, deeply influenced me. With so many others, I am exceptionally grateful for his wild life.

Resources

One way I have sought to give back for what I learned from Foreman and those he inspired and battled is by writing about them and also letting them speak for themselves. With Foreman's permission, for example, and with the generous support of the Rachel Carson Center in Munich, Germany, I curated a virtual exhibition that digitized all the issues of *Earth First!* published with Dave Foreman at the helm (including after John Davis took over), and after they departed, as well as the journal *Wild Earth*. See: Bron Taylor, "Radical Environmentalism's Print History: From *Earth First!* to *Wild Earth*." Environment & Society Portal, *Virtual Exhibitions* 2018, no. 1. Rachel Carson Center for Environment and Society. doi.org/10.5282/rcc/7988.

My first book about the movement was *Ecological Resistance Movements: The Global Emergence of Radical and Popular Environmentalism*, which I edited and was published by the State University of New York Press in 1995. I have published many more articles about radical and grassroots environmentalism, deep ecology, and ecocentric philosophy and spirituality; these are searchable and downloadable at http://brontaylor.com/102-2/publications/published-by-subject/. For a book that pays significant attention to Dave Foreman and other radical environmentalists, and shows the growing cultural traction of what I have elsewhere called 'spiritualities of belonging and connection to nature,' see *Dark Green Religion: Nature Spirituality and the Planetary Future*, which was published by the University of California Press in 2010. The quotations from Dave Foreman are cited in my previously published work.

Bron Taylor is Professor of Religion and Environmental Ethics at the University of Florida, a Fellow of the Rachel Carson Center for Environment and Society at Ludwig-Maximilians-Universität, Munich, Germany, and a Senior Research Scholar at the Leibniz-Institut für Europäische Geschichte at the University of Mainz, Germany. An interdisciplinary environmental studies scholar, Taylor's research explores through the lenses of the sciences and humanities the complex relationships of religion, ecology, ethics, and the quest for sustainability. His books include *Dark Green Religion:*

Nature Spirituality and the Planetary Future (2010), *Avatar and Nature Spirituality* (2013), and *Ecological Resistance Movements* (1995). He is also editor of the *Encyclopedia of Religion and Nature* (2005). In 2017, he received a Lifetime Achievement award from the International Society for the Study of Religion, Nature, and Culture. For publications, interviews, and more, see www.brontaylor.com. His Twitter venue is @BronTaylor.

Dave speaking at 50th Anniversary Wilderness Act gathering © Amy Gulick/amygulick.com

A Great One for the Ages

Louisa Wilcox

(Written by Louisa after she received notice of Dave's passing.)

Bart and Howie introduced me to Dave in 1981. I had driven all night from Jackson with Howie (maybe Roselle too?) to Lake Foul, where I met some of the craziest and most inspired bunch of dirtbag earth defenders I have ever had the privilege of crashing in the dirt with—Dave among the bravest.

In my geezerhood, many memories tend to smush together, but those early days with you gonzo bastards in 4 Corners and other wilds are as clear as the night sky was when Spurs, you, and I sought what had to have been a new route out of the Maze. Or when Dave, Howie, I, and others swam parts of the flooded Paria River. Near misses, as so many adventures were with this wild bunch.

Some of the most important lessons about life, daring, and what it means to stand up for Mother Nature I learned from Dave—and you all.

May he rest in peace—and may we find a way to get together to celebrate his life and honor his indomitable spirit.

– Louisa

Louisa Willcox is the founder of *Grizzly Times*. Working for Natural Resources Defense Council, Sierra Club, Center for Biological Diversity, and Greater Yellowstone Coalition, Louisa has advocated for grizzly bear preservation for over 30 years. She specializes in developing comprehensive strategies that succeed because they work on multiple scales using various approaches, including grassroots organizing and outreach, education, media and communication, policy analysis, lobbying, coalition development, and public protest. She and a handful of others have prevented Yellowstone grizzly bear delisting for over two decades. Louisa has a BA from Williams College and a Master's of Forest Policy from the Yale School of Forestry and Environmental Studies. In 2014, she was given a lifetime achievement award from Yale.

Afterword: Happy Trails

Dave Foreman left us too soon—he had much work left to do. As the testimonials in this collection attest, he was certainly not alone in his nearly lifelong effort to protect wild places and wildeors. He knew he could not do what needed doing in his lifetime, or by himself, and one of his greatest accomplishments was to help build an army of conservationists to carry on the work that needed doing. The crises he saw, and the urgency he felt to respond, grew over his career. While he knew he had done all he could, he was discouraged in his last years. The world did not seem to be responding to his calls for action. But was that the case?

When one has a grand vision, as Dave described in *Rewilding North America*, frustration at slow progress toward large and complex goals is probably inevitable. He felt such frustration but kept working, even as family tragedy and health problems sapped his energy. He could not be content with a situation in which the problems that concerned him are not solved, and what he saw as existential problems like loss of biodiversity and climate change seemed far from getting the attention they deserved. Dave was a man of action. He was impatient. He held strong views and believed that he was right most of the time, though he could admit to having been wrong or even overwrought at times. He had, according to long-time friends, mellowed over the decades, but not too much.

The world is changing. Dave coined the term "rewilding" and, as several here attest, it has gained traction far beyond what he could reasonably expect when it occurred to him. It has become a worldwide movement, building on the momentum of rapidly growing recognition of the consequences of biodiversity loss. No grand scheme for rewilding North America has been funded or grown politically popular, but the serious discussion of 30X30 and Nature Needs Half is underway across the world, and Dave contributed to those discussions. History will recognize his contributions.

Dave was no paragon of virtue, as he would readily admit. Like everyone, he had his difficulties and blind spots. He suffered great ups and downs and joked that every time he had a major crisis he started a new organization—and there was some truth to that. He could be a difficult collaborator, but as many here testify, he got things done. He was inspirational, a very hard worker, an uncompromising advocate. He was much loved. Wild places and wildeors, along with his wife Nancy, were the loves of his life. Hiking boots, rafts, canoes, even scuba tanks, carried him to his earthly Nirvana. He told friends that once, feeling threatened by a musk ox in the Arctic, he felt ready to go. Dying in a wild place because he had foolishly underestimated the power of a wildeor seemed to him not only a proper way to depart this life but also divine justice.

So, Dave will be sorely missed, but his work will continue. The challenge for those veterans of his campaigns who remain is to see that a new generation seizes the mantle of conservation with a measure of the passion that so characterized Smilodon Dave, Uncle Bumblefuss, the fierce ecowarrior.

Dave Has the Last Word

Tackling the crash of the Tree of Life, wild-loving conservationists are putting into words and deed a new dream for North America, one in which true wilderness and the wildeor can live with a healthy human civilization. This vision is bold, scientifically believable, workable, and *hopeful*. I emphasize hopefulness because I have found that all kinds of folks in the United States and Canada answer wholeheartedly to the hope underlying the North American Wildlands Network. I believe that this vision, as the heart of a conservation strategy for North America, tied to other steps in this and the chapter before, can take back and breathe new life into the wilderness and wildlife network. And it can wake up North Americans to come together as good, thoughtful, caring citizens of the land community and work to do things right. Rewilding a North American Wildlands Network is the soul of true citizenship for the Twenty-first Century. It won't work, however, if we water it down by leaving out wolves and big cats so as not to frighten the wealthy and mighty, the dullards and the quaking-hearted.

Once again, I find myself at the end of a book, where I should start singing "Zippity doo dah, zippity ay, my oh my what a wonderful day!" And, once again, I can't do it. We face deep, dark days ahead. There are no wizards with drylic answers. No Mount Dooms in which to throw the evil ring of Sauron. No otherworldly park rangers in flying saucers are going to come zooming in to hand out citations to Mankind and make us follow the rules for a healthy Earth Galactic Park, much as I may daydream.

But I can say this: Shielders and keepers of wild things and wild Earth can stand up, take back the conservation network, step up to the looming dread forthrightly, bring population stabilization to the fore once again, and work like hell for a *hopeful* vision of wildeors and true wilderness side by side with a caring civilization. We cannot fail to stand up in this do-or-die, eleventh hour for thriving, thronging, and manyfold dazzle of all life and the unfathomable evolutionary tomorrow.

– Dave Foreman
Take Back Conservation

Acknowledgements

We have many to thank for contributing to the Dave Foreman Legacy Project, of which *Wildeor* is a part. Foremost among them are those who contributed tributes to this memorial publication. John Davis and David Johns checked the editor's connecting sections for accuracy, and Reed Noss clarified the Half Earth portion. Jack Lustig and Liz Mercuri at Fine Arts New Mexico contributed their skill and expertise to digitize the photographs. Jack Loeffler provided invaluable literary counseling to John and Susan. Jack Humphrey performed Artificial Intelligence magic with photographs that were of lower resolution. George Davis and Katie Shepard at Essex Editions made the publication possible, contributing in many ways to its excellence. Dave Foreman's sister Roxanne Pacheco was supportive throughout, making invaluable resources available to the editors, and Nancy's sisters Lynn and Marie supported Dave and Nancy and helped with end-of-life details. Dave and Nancy loved their cats, Misty and Yampa, who helped everyone who came to their house during this transition.

The Rewilding Institute provided financial support for the publication, as did George Davis. Another part of the Legacy Project has been the archiving of Dave Foreman's papers, most of which are awaiting archivist attention at the Denver Public Library (DPL) in the Dave Foreman Collection of its remarkable Conservation History Collection. Many thanks to the DPL staff, especially Jaimie Seemiller, who will be making Dave's voluminous papers accessible to researchers who are studying the conservation episodes of which Dave was a significant part. Christianne Hinks deserves special thanks for her untiring work to get the papers to the DPL. We, the editors, thank all who encouraged us in this project.

Smilodon Fatalis © *Susan Morgan*

CPSIA information can be obtained
at www.ICGtesting.com
Printed in the USA
LVHW070038120623
749470LV00006B/737

9 781733 519045